WEEP
MORE:

A BOOK FOR THOSE WHO SORROW

DAN SARDINAS

© 2024, Dan Sardinas. All rights reserved.

ISBN 9798878131902

Unless otherwise indicated, all Scripture quotations are from The Holy Bible, English Standard Version® (ESV®), copyright © 2001 by Crossway, a publishing ministry of Good News Publishers. Used by permission. All rights reserved.

ACKNOWLEDGMENTS

I would like to express my sincere appreciation to a group of special people who reviewed my book before it was published.

I am grateful for Lori Sardinas, Debbie Perry, Donna Hebert, Randall Miller, Brenda Vann, and Michael Maginness for their hard work in providing feedback and guidance throughout the book's development. May God use your contributions to bless and help many people who are struggling with their sorrows.

ABOUT THE AUTHOR

Dan is married to Lori, and they have three adult children (Tyler, Brianna, and Brandon). Dan has been in pastoral ministry for 25 years. He has served as a pastor of the Northwest Baptist Church in Bradenton, Florida since 2013. Dan has authored other self-published works which he has written for his church family. Some of these works can be found on Amazon.com.

Gospel Confusion: Confessions of a Pastor (2012)
40 Days of Light (2013)
50 Days of Promise (2014)
Grace upon Grace (2015)
Breath upon Breath (2016)
Glory upon Glory (2017)
The One: A Christmas Devotional (2020)
The Two: Shadows of the Gospel (2021)
The Five: Solas of the Reformation (2022)
The Servant of the Lord (2022)
Pursuing Holiness (with various authors) (2023)
Weep No More: A Book For Those Who Sorrow (2024)

For more information about Dan Sardinas and Northwest Baptist Church, visit www.nwbcbradenton.org, where you can hear his sermons and learn more about the church he calls home.

CONTENTS

ABOUT THE AUTHOR..................................4
CHAPTER 1: THE CONQUEROR FOR WEEPING 7
CHAPTER 2: THE PURPOSE OF WEEPING........20
CHAPTER 3: THE GOOD OF WEEPING..............32
CHAPTER 4: THE JOURNEY OF WEEPING 46
CHAPTER 5: ANXIETY AND WEEPING...............59
CHAPTER 6: FAILURE AND WEEPING.................71
CHAPTER 7: RELATIONSHIPS AND WEEPING.86
CHAPTER 8: JUSTICE AND WEEPING 97
CHAPTER 9: DEATH AND WEEPING..................109
CHAPTER 10: PRAYER AND WEEPING.............123
CHAPTER 11: BETRAYAL AND WEEPING........136
CHAPTER 12: REPENTANCE AND WEEPING .148
CHAPTER 13: GUILT AND WEEPING.................163
CHAPTER 14: THE END OF WEEPING? 177

6

CHAPTER 1:
THE CONQUEROR FOR WEEPING

According to church tradition, the Apostle John was persecuted by being boiled in oil.[1] After surviving this ordeal, John was banished to a Roman penal colony on the isle of Patmos. Patmos is an island in the Aegean Sea, near modern-day Turkey's coast. We know he was on Patmos because he tells us so at the beginning of Revelation. *"I, John, your brother and partner in the tribulation and the kingdom and the patient endurance that are in Jesus, was on the island called Patmos on account of the word of God and the testimony of Jesus." (Revelation 1:9)* While John was on Patmos, he received a vision from the Lord Jesus, which was to be given to seven churches in Asia Minor. Why did Jesus give John this revelation? It is not the reason many would suspect.

Today, many are absorbed into prophecy charts and timelines that pinpoint with speculation the timing, nature, and characters of the last days. It is essential to understand that Revelation was not written so that we could debate the details of the apocalypse. The purpose of Revelation is woven throughout each verse of this mysterious letter in symbols and Old Testament

---

[1] *Tertullian, The Prescription Against Heretics, Ch 36 (as found on https://www.newadvent.org/fathers/0311.htm)*

imagery. The main message of Revelation is hope so that the church would be encouraged amid their suffering. It was so that they would remain steadfast as they got a vision of a triumphant Christ, who is the King of kings and the Lord of lords. Revelation is the good news that although the world is falling apart, Jesus wins. William Hendrickson says this help and comfort would come as God gives them the "assurance that God sees their tears."[2] The hope is that during their great tribulation, Jesus is with them. *"For the Lamb in the midst of the throne will be their shepherd, and he will guide them to springs of living water, and God will wipe away every tear from their eyes." (Revelation 7:17)* God saw the tears of these persecuted saints, and this would have been a great comfort to these first recipients of this letter. Their persecution and deaths would not be for nothing. By professing Christ even unto death, they were sealing the fate of God's enemies on earth.

Revelation was written during a time of severe persecution for the church. The Roman emperors Nero and Domitian ruled Rome during the Apostles' time. The Roman historian Tacitus gave a detailed account of Nero's cruel reign of terror in Book XV of his *Annals*. Nero was by far the worst of the emperors and induced much suffering at the expense of the church. He was a wicked man who manipulated people to accomplish his

---

[2] *Hendrickson, pg 14*

goals, even if it meant lying, murder, and thievery. It is said that Nero once set fire to the city of Rome (because he wanted to build a new palace) but then used the Christians as scapegoats.[3] It was this that led to much suffering for these early Christians. Christians were thrown to wild beasts to be eaten for sport for the pleasure of spectators.[4] Christians were also beheaded, pierced with swords and spears, set on fire, cut in half, sewn alive in animal skins that were dipped in oil, used as human torches to light the streets, and, yes, even crucified.

There was much to weep about in the first-century church as it seemed that Christians were losing just by the widespread persecution. However, nothing could be further from the truth. Persecution did not extinguish the fire of the gospel, but it only spread it all the more. Even then, 1st-century Christians were living at a time when they could be persecuted and killed any day. Through their blood, the gospel continued to spread like wildfire. As Tertullian once famously said, "The blood of the martyrs is the seed of the church."[5] Therefore, the Lord gave John the Revelation to

---

[3] *https://www.livius.org/sources/content/tacitus/tacitus-on-the-christians/*

[4] *https://brians.wsu.edu/2016/11/14/tacitus-neros-persecution-of-the-christians/*

[5] *"The Apology," Latin Christianity: Its Founder, Tertullian, Roberts, A., Donaldson, J., and Coxe, A. C., ed., Thelwall, S., trans., vol. 3, The Ante-Nicene Fathers, Christian Literature Company, 1885, p. 55).*

encourage believers until he returns. Revelation was written so that those living in the first century would be "blessed" by God's promises. This is what John says about Revelation, *"Blessed is the one who reads aloud the words of this prophecy, and blessed are those who hear, and who keep what is written in it, for the time is near." (Revelation 1:3)* John told his readers that those who hear and keep what is written will be "blessed." The Greek word for blessed is the same word for "happy."[6] Revelation was not written to scare the people of God; it was meant to bless them. Understanding what the early church had to endure for the gospel's sake makes even more sense as to its purpose. Through John, Jesus addressed the seven churches directly. He did this by addressing them with both rebukes and affirmations of his love. The Lord knows that difficult days lay ahead for his people, and he wants them prepared for what is to come as the gospel triumphs around the world.

In Revelation 4, through a vision, John is invited into heaven through an open door. Upon entering the door, he saw a throne and God seated upon it. In chapter 5, John describes a scene too glorious for mere words. He saw someone sitting on the throne holding a scroll in his hand, but John noted

---

[6] *Arndt, William, Frederick W. Danker, Walter Bauer, and F. Wilbur Gingrich. 2000. In A Greek-English Lexicon of the New Testament and Other Early Christian Literature, 3rd ed., 610. Chicago: University of Chicago Press.*

11

that it was sealed with seven seals. Seven seals on one scroll? What is in this scroll? What could be so important? This scroll is vital to those in attendance as they eagerly await someone to open it. What is the significance of a scroll with seals? According to Ligonier ministries, "In the ancient world, messages were commonly written on scrolls that were then rolled up and tied with a string. Dollops of hot wax were then put on the string, and the sender of a message and witnesses would press their signets into the wax, creating impressions that authenticated the message and proved that it was from the one who was identified as its author. One could unroll the scroll and read it only if the seals were broken, but not just anyone could break the seal. Only the addressee had the authority to break the seal."[7]

    The angel then asks, *"Who is worthy to open the scroll and break its seals?" (Revelation 5:2)* John doesn't take this as good news. If the angel doesn't know who is worthy of opening the scroll, then he never will. Will he ever discover what's in this scroll? John becomes upset at the thought of not knowing this vital information. He begins to worry that nobody will be found worthy. He comments by saying, *"And no one in heaven or on earth or under the earth was able to open the scroll or to look into it and I began to weep loudly because no one was found worthy to*

---

[7] *https://www.ligonier.org/learn/devotionals/the-scroll-with-seven-seals*

open the scroll or to look into it." (Revelation 5:3) I believe John wept because he anticipated relief for his brothers and sisters on the earth. He had just seen the Lord Jesus on Patmos before coming into this heavenly vision. Jesus had promised "happy" news of things that would happen soon. However, now that no one was found able to open up this scroll, will the suffering never end? John does the only thing that comes naturally to him: he weeps. This word for weep that John uses in Greek is a crushing blow to the soul. The emphasis was on an audible sound that came with his tears.[8] John wailed in severe disappointment. John wasn't merely disappointed; he was devastated at the news and audibly cried. John said, *"I began to weep loudly."* Have you ever been there? Have you ever needed some good news, but it's nowhere to be found? Have you ever been expecting some news that you thought would give you relief, but in the end, it never came? That's how John felt in this moment before the throne of God and this heavenly host. However, John's weeping was short-lived, for John reports, *"And one of the elders said to me, '**Weep no more;** behold, the Lion of the tribe of Judah, the Root of David, has conquered, so that he can open the scroll and its seven seals." (Revelation 5:5)*

---

[8] *Lust, Johan, Erik Eynikel, and Katrin Hauspie. 2003. In <u>A Greek-English Lexicon of the Septuagint : Revised Edition</u>. Deutsche Bibelgesellschaft: Stuttgart.*

13

Weep no more! This is the news that John needed to hear but didn't expect. I'm sure John hoped the church's suffering would end then, but it didn't. Despite the current suffering, John, there is a new truth to behold and one that you can take to your grave. John, you can stop weeping now, for someone is worthy to open that scroll. That scroll doesn't yet contain the end of your suffering, but it will one day. The scroll being opened is the beginning of the end, and that beginning begins now. You won't have to wait for this to be true, John. John, this is not something for people living in the 2000s to decipher codes about, but it will be true for the rest of time. The fifth seal has John's answer. John sees the souls of those who had been slain for their testimony for Jesus. They are John's persecuted brothers and sisters in Christ. The answer to when the suffering will end was not fully answered, but it's enough for John.

What was so encouraging about that fifth seal? John says, *"When he opened the fifth seal, I saw under the altar the souls of those who had been slain for the word of God and for the witness they had borne. They cried out with a loud voice, 'O Sovereign Lord, holy and true, how long before you will judge and avenge our blood on those who dwell on the earth?' Then they were each given a white robe and told to rest a little longer, until the number of their fellow servants and their brothers should be complete, who were to be killed as they themselves had been." (Revelation 6:9–11)*

The answer John needed to hear was now given. The suffering would not end just yet but would continue until all who were to be martyred would die. Yes, John, more believers will die and be slaughtered. However, don't worry about them, for all those slain are at rest now until a future time. The *"souls under the altar"* are all those who have been martyred for Christ. God didn't entirely give John the answer he expected, but he did give John the answer he needed and the answer that we need today. The promises of God are sufficient for our weeping.

John, the reason you can "weep no more" is that there is someone who can open those seals. Even though your suffering will not end now, there is a day in which it will. John, the best news is that you know the One who can open these seals. Who is it? It is the *"Lion of the tribe of Judah; the root of David."* These are titles of the Messiah! The Lion of the tribe of Judah was prophesied in Genesis 49:9-10. This happened when Jacob was blessing his sons before his death. He came to Judah and said, *"Judah is a lion's cub; from the prey, my son, you have gone up. He stooped down; he crouched as a lion and as a lioness; who dares rouse him? The scepter shall not depart from Judah, nor the ruler's staff from between his feet, until tribute comes to him; and to him shall be the obedience of the peoples." (Genesis 49:9-10)* The Messiah was to come from the Tribe of Judah! The Messiah was also to come from the root of David. This, of course, is about

Isaiah's prophecy about whose lineage Messiah would come through (see Isaiah 11:1-5). John would have known what these titles meant and who is worthy enough to open the seals and end the suffering.

How did he conquer? John then sees something else, *"And between the throne and the four living creatures and among the elders I saw a Lamb standing, as though it had been slain…" (Revelation 5:6)* This is someone that John recognizes! This is the Lamb of God! This is Jesus, who had been crucified and had risen again. He is not lying in a grave; He is not hanging on a cross; He is standing in victory! John then hears them sing a new song. *"And they sang a new song, saying, 'Worthy are you to take the scroll and to open its seals, for you were slain, and by your blood you ransomed people for God from every tribe and language and people and nation, and you have made them a kingdom and priests to our God, and they shall reign on the earth." (Revelation 5:9-10)*

The Lamb conquered by being slain! By being slain, he conquered by purchasing the people of God from all tribes, nations, and languages. It is for this reason that He is worthy to open the scrolls. For it is in His obedience unto death that He has done what is necessary to redeem people to God that will ultimately end their suffering. I'm sure this reminded John of what he heard Jesus say in chapter 1. *"Fear not, I am the first and the last, and the living one. I died, and behold I am alive forevermore, and I have the keys of Death and Hades." (Revelation 1:18)* Jesus is alive although he was slain. Jesus has the keys of death, although he was dead. Yes, this is a reason to weep no more.

Oh, but it's still not over, for John heard the worship and praise for the Lamb continue. *"Then I looked, and I heard around the throne and the living creatures and the elders the voice of many angels, numbering myriads of myriads and thousands of thousands, saying with a loud voice, 'Worthy is the Lamb who was slain, to receive power and wealth and wisdom and might and honor and glory and blessing!' And I heard every creature in heaven and on earth and under the earth and in the sea, and all that is in them, saying, 'To him who sits on the throne and to the Lamb be blessing and honor and glory and might forever and ever!' And the four living creatures said, 'Amen!' and the elders fell down and worshiped." (Revelation 5:11–14)*

What is in these seals? There is much debate over the meaning and significance of the vision Jesus gave to John. However, let's just say that it's good news. It's good news for the people of God that these seals are opened. God hasn't promised an easy road. He has not promised us flowery beds of ease. However, he promised us that our sorrow wouldn't last forever. John, this is why you can weep no more. Your sorrows will vanish like an iceberg on the sun's surface. All suffering points to this moment in history. Our heartaches, tears, grief, and diseases find resolution in this worthy Lamb who can open the scroll and break its seals because He has conquered. In the remaining chapters of Revelation, John hears of Jesus' victory over beasts, dragons, and serpents as His kingdom conquers. John, it may seem as if the emperor is winning, but He doesn't win.

John's weeping over this scroll to open is also echoed in our deepest hurts and longings. John's weeping was for the end of it all and for Jesus' victory to be seen on earth. Yes, and that, my friends, is the answer we also must seek for every pain in our hearts. In this book, we will explore some ways we weep, why we weep, the benefits of weeping, and why Jesus is the answer. Our suffering is ongoing, but it won't always be like this. So, even though we can weep now, we rest in the fact that there is coming a day in which we won't. Why? For Jesus Christ has conquered. He has conquered by dying on the cross for our sins, by being buried in a tomb, and by being raised to life three days later. After each chapter, I will remind you of the glorious truth of the Lamb's conquest as the balm for your weary souls. Hang tight; Jesus sits on his throne until he makes all his enemies his footstool. He is coming again! Weep no more!

Although you feel as if your pain will never end,
Let me give you some assurance, my friend,
The Lion of the Tribe of Judah has won the war,
And for this reason, you will one day weep no more.

DISCUSSION QUESTIONS

1. Can you relate to John's sense of disappointment or despair in any aspect of your life? How does the promise of Jesus' ultimate victory over suffering offer you hope in those moments?

2. How does the image of Jesus as the conquering Lamb bring you comfort in your current circumstances? How does knowing that Jesus has overcome the world impact your outlook on life's sorrows?

3. Why do you think weeping is such a significant theme in the Bible, especially in the context of suffering and persecution? How does weeping relate to our human experience and our need for comfort and hope?

4. How does the promise of God wiping away every tear (Revelation 7:17) give you hope during life's challenges and sorrows? How can you trust in God's comforting presence during times of weeping?

CHAPTER 2:
THE PURPOSE OF WEEPING

Everyone cries. Tears are natural to the human experience. In a sense, our eyes always have some tears in them. The most common types of tears are the ones that keep our eyeballs moist; they are called basal tears.[9] Some tears protect our eyes from irritants like smoke or onions and are called reflex tears. Our tears can be triggered by feeling pain in our bodies or perhaps by being nostalgic and sentimental. However, the most common tears, which will be the focus of this book, come from our emotions. These emotional tears flush out stress hormones and other toxins from our system.[10] Humans cry for a multitude of reasons. We cry when times are good (tears of joy) or bad (tears of sorrow). No matter the reason for our tears, I believe that crying is a gift from God to express our emotions. There is something very therapeutic about crying, and I have even heard some say, "I just needed a good cry."

Many men, and some women, struggle with expressing their emotions. Some men consider tears to be a sign of weakness or even a sign that they are being too effeminate. It is then that I like to remind them that God gave them tears for a reason. It is of no use to

---

[9] *https://www.allaboutvision.com/eye-care/eye-anatomy/what-are-tears-made-of/*

[10] *https://www.health.harvard.edu/blog/is-crying-good-for-you-2021030122020*

hold your tears back. You aren't stronger if you don't cry. The manliest man who ever lived cried more than once. *"Jesus wept." (John 11:35)* If it's okay for Jesus to cry, then it's okay for us to cry (see also Luke 19:41-42, Hebrews 5:7). So please, by all means, let the waterworks flow! Some of us are more emotional than others; as the old expression goes, some "wear their emotions on their sleeves." When God has given us a gift, we must use it for its intended purpose. Tears are a gift from God and a way to deal with the pains of a broken and sinful world. Therefore, crying or weeping does have its God-given place in our lives. Those who would disagree and say that we shouldn't cry deny the Scripture, for Solomon said that there is *"a time to weep." (Ecclesiastes 3:4)*

As a pastor, I have done my fair share of counseling and have seen countless tears flow down the cheeks of many people as they share their sorrows or sins. For this reason, I try to keep a box of tissues near my desk. I have found that many people try to hold back or fight those tears. However, that is one of the worst things that someone can do. To hold back tears may seem courageous to others, but it is not always helpful to the person who has these emotions bottled up. When we try not to cry in front of others, it most likely stems from pride in our hearts. Not rightfully expressing emotion can be likened to never emptying the garbage can in your kitchen. Your garbage can was meant to hold only so much, but once it is full, it must be emptied before the house is filled with ungodly odors. Tears allow us to express emotion and empty our hearts before God. God didn't give us tears and emotions by accident.

Why, then, do we cry? If tears are a gift of God, then why are they associated with so much pain? Pain doesn't sound like a good gift. Our sorrows are symptomatic of a deeper problem that makes our tears necessary. Pain is not necessarily a gift of God, as it is a consequence of being sinners. Even though it is natural for us to feel sorrow, it was not so initially. Adam and Eve rebelled against God's law and fell from their original state of innocence. God had warned them, *"You may surely eat of every tree of the garden, but of the tree of the knowledge of good and evil you shall not eat, for in the day that you eat of it you shall surely die." (Genesis 2:15–17)* Even though creation was still in its infancy, nothing had ever died or experienced pain. Until then, there had never been any sorrow or anything to be sad about. However, when they chose to sin against God and obey the serpent, everything changed. Because of their sinful actions, God cursed Adam and Eve. Their sin made a world of pain, suffering, and sorrow a reality. Why, then, do we cry? Well, tears are just a way for our souls to long for another world, a perfect world. This is a pathway we must all travel as it is expected as a part of the human experience. Charles Spurgeon said it this way, "The road to sorrow has been well trodden, it is the regular sheep track to heaven, and all the flock of God have had to pass along it."[11]

Spurgeon, who is known as the "Prince of Preachers," experienced a lifetime of sorrow and depression. That might surprise some of you who would never consider such a giant of the faith to have lived a sorrowful life, but it is true. Spurgeon experienced a life-changing event when a prankster yelled "fire" during a church service. This sent the crowded room into a panic, leaving seven dead and twenty-eight badly injured.[12] His wife, Susannah, even once remarked about his sorrow, "My beloved's anguish was so deep and violent, that reason seemed to totter in his throne, and we sometimes feared that he would never preach again."[13] This event sent Spurgeon into a state of sadness for the rest of his life. Yes, even the godliest men suffer the effects of a fallen world. This is true because they are also fallen in Adam.

Staying upon the "mountain of joy" every waking second in this world is impossible. Even though

---

[11] *Charles Spurgeon, "The Fainting Hero," MTP, Vol. 55.*

[12] *https://www.crossway.org/articles/did-you-know-that-charles-spurgeon-struggled-with-depression/*

[13] *Charles Ray, "The Life of Susannah Spurgeon," in Morning Devotions by Susannah Spurgeon: Free Grace and Dying Love (Edinburgh: Banner of Truth, 2006), 166.*

unrealistic and unbiblical, it is still the false message preached by the "Word of Faith" and the prosperity gospel movement. One of the many travesties to come out of this false teaching is the rejection of suffering and sorrow. This movement considers all sorrow and sickness beyond God's will for life. This is simply not true, as even a brief survey of the Scriptures shows how God uses suffering and sorrow and even ordains it. This false teaching is so damaging to those who struggle with pain, sickness, and various griefs. This kind of false teaching has been popularized by false teachers such as Bill Johnson from Bethel Church in Redding, California. Johnson believes that it's always God's will for a person to be healed, so he believes sickness and sorrow are outside the realm of God's will. He misinterprets Jesus' words "on earth as it is in heaven" to justify this belief.

In his book The Way of Life, Johnson wrote, "Simply put, there is no sickness there, so there is to be none here. There is no torment or sin in Heaven, so there is to be none here. We should never again question God's will in a given situation, if in fact it involves sin, sickness, or torment. It may be challenging but it's not complicated."[14] Johnson fails to provide any exegetical evidence as to why this phrase in Jesus' prayer and the great commission is to be merged. Since

---

[14] Johnson, Bill, The Presence of God, , 2018 Destiny Image Publishers, Kindle

he believes it's always God's will to heal, he then puts the blame on the person for his "lack of faith." Do you see how that can be so damaging? The sufferer is then deceived into thinking, "What's wrong with me? Why is there no healing for me?" He then carries the burden of his healing, making it an idol he worships. This leads to more sorrow and despair as the person has no hope for a healing that will never come in this life. "Simply put" Johnson's theology lays an even heavier burden on the shoulders of the one who sorrows.

    I believe that Johnson's false teaching suffers from an over-realized eschatology. He desires good and great things — no sin, sickness, and suffering. Who wouldn't desire that? However, he fails to see that this is the future reality of the new heavens and the new earth and is not possible in the age in which we live now. God has promised us that he will make all things new, and that one day we will experience a great resurrection from this sin-cursed world (see Revelation 21:1-4). I don't think I have to convince anyone that sin, sickness, and suffering continue in this present world. It is not our calling to eliminate sickness — King Jesus does that through his glorious appearing. This is not to say that we are not to pray for healing, for God does indeed heal. However, this earth is not heaven yet. God does provide deliverance from these things when it is according to his will. However, as we will see, God is sovereign even over our sorrows and is good even when no healing exists.

Why does there have to be tears? What is the purpose of crying? How can a good God allow all this sorrow? It's not God's fault. Sin has separated us from God, causing all sorts of sadness, pain, and misery. Almost every sorrow you've ever felt had to do with some sin, either in your life or another person's life. This curse brought upon humanity was given to Adam, Eve, and the serpent. First, God spoke with Eve, *"I will surely multiply your pain in childbearing; in pain, you shall bring forth children. Your desire shall be contrary to your husband, but he shall rule over you." And to Adam, he said, "Because you have listened to the voice of your wife and have eaten of the tree of which I commanded you, 'You shall not eat of it,' cursed is the ground because of you; in pain you shall eat of it all the days of your life; thorns and thistles it shall bring forth for you; and you shall eat the plants of the field. By the sweat of your face, you shall eat bread, till you return to the ground, for out of it you were taken; for you are dust, and to dust you shall return." (Genesis 3:16–19)* This curse would not die with them but would continue in every generation. *"Therefore, just as sin came into the world through one man, and death through sin, and so death spread to all men because all sinned." (Romans 5:12)* Adam and Eve began a deluge of tears growing throughout history, affecting every human. Another way to illustrate this is what I heard John Piper recently say. He said, "This world is a conveyor belt of disappointments."[15]

It is not a sin to sorrow. Even our Savior was a *"man of sorrows and acquainted with grief"* (Isaiah 53:3). This doesn't mean that Jesus lived a depressed life. It means that Jesus took on our sorrows because he took on our sins. It is no wonder that as the Father's cup of wrath was being poured out upon him while on the cross, he cried, *"My God, my God, why have you forsaken me?" (Matthew 27:46)* Sin brings pain, sadness, and yes, even death. This is why, just moments later, *"Jesus cried out again with a loud voice and yielded up his spirit." (Matthew 27:50)* Jesus took on human flesh to experience something he could not have experienced otherwise—death. This suffering is what Isaiah prophesied the Messiah would do, *"Surely he has borne our griefs and carried our sorrows; yet we esteemed him stricken, smitten by God, and afflicted. But he was pierced for our transgressions; he was crushed for our iniquities; upon him was the chastisement that brought us peace, and with his wounds, we are healed." (Isaiah 53:4–5)*

We must learn to weep and see our tears as the gift they are intended to be. Puritan pastor John Flavel wrote a beneficial book entitled *A Token for Mourners*. It has been reprinted today under the title *Facing Grief*. He

---
[15] *From the Q&A panel at Shepherd's Conference 2024*

wrote this book after experiencing his wife's death. Flavel also tragically mourned and wept over the death of his six children. In total, Flavel had nine children, but only three of them survived into adulthood. Flavel explores the depths of grief and how one should see it in one's life. The one thing that Flavel wrote, which was indelibly impressed upon me, was our desire for our grief to end. Flavel wisely wrote, "Desire not to be delivered from your sorrows one moment before God's time. Let patience have its perfect work; that comfort, which comes in God's way and season, may remain and do you good."[16] That is quite a humbling statement to think and ponder through. The one thing we all agree about sorrow is we want it to run its course as swiftly as possible. Who doesn't want his grief to end? Any honest person would like to be relieved of sorrow immediately. The answer, of course, is that none of us wants to grieve. None of us wants to feel sad or be filled with sorrow. However, if we see our tears as a gift from God, we will view it far differently. God is good and will not let us suffer beyond his will. He is sovereign despite our sorrow and suffering and will end it when he has accomplished its purpose. If our sorrow is a gift from God to express our heart, then we must let it accomplish what God has sent it to accomplish. This requires great faith to see that God is not distant

---

[16] Flavel, John, *Facing Grief*, The Banner of Truth Trust, Carlisle, PA, 2017, xxi

from our pain.

God has a purpose for your sorrows and knows all about them. He is good to you despite your grief. He is kind to you despite the perceived delay in answering your prayers. He is gracious to you not to let you walk alone. Even though others may not know the pain within, take great comfort knowing that not one teardrop escapes God's notice. The Psalmist gives us great hope in this way when he says, *"You have kept count of my tossings; put my tears in your bottle. Are they not in your book?" (Psalm 56:8)* The Psalmist speaks like this to remind himself that with God there are no wasted tears. He knows about every tear before it leaves your eyes. God sees, hears, notices, cares, and is near. He once answered Hezekiah's prayer by saying, *"Thus says the Lord, the God of David your father: I have heard your prayer; I have seen your tears. Behold, I will heal you." (2 Kings 20:5)*

When will it end? Why does it have to continue to be like this? I don't have all those answers; I wish I did. There is a purpose, and it is not for nothing. I can promise you that God will deliver you from all your troubles. What the Psalmist says here is true. *"When the righteous cry for help, the LORD hears and delivers them out of all their troubles. The LORD is near to the brokenhearted and saves the crushed in spirit. Many are the afflictions of the righteous, but the LORD delivers him out of them all." (Psalm 34:17-19)*

This does not mean that all of our troubles disappear in this life, but they will vanish one day. However, the promise is that even though God doesn't take our pain away in this life, he is near to us and saves us. We desire that our pain disappear in this life, but if God allows it to remain, there is a purpose. If it does remain, know that this life is nothing compared to eternity. This brief life doesn't even appear as a blip on the radar of history. I may not know if your sorrow will be eased in this life. However, I do know this: it will end. The tears that are a gift now in this life will no longer be necessary. There is much promise that our weeping will soon turn into joy. *"Weeping may tarry for the night, but joy comes with the morning." (Psalm 30:5)*

Hang on, for it will be soon, friends. Soon.

Although you feel as if your pain will never end,
Let me give you some assurance, my friend,
The Lion of the Tribe of Judah has won the war,
And for this reason, you will one day weep no more.

DISCUSSION QUESTIONS

1. Discuss the idea that tears are a gift from God. How does this perspective change the way we view and experience sorrow?

2. Why do you think crying is often viewed as a sign of weakness, especially among men? How can this perception be changed?

3. Reflect on the idea that holding back tears is akin to never emptying the garbage can in your kitchen. How does this analogy resonate with you, and how can we ensure that we allow ourselves to fully express our emotions? When was the last time you emptied your "garbage can?"

4. In what ways can Jesus' own tears and sorrows (e.g., John 11:35, Luke 19:41-42) inspire us to embrace our own emotions and express them authentically before God and others?

5. How does the Word of Faith movement's teaching on pain, sickness, and sorrow hurt people? Have you experienced deception from this movement? What counsel would you offer someone stuck in this hole?

CHAPTER 3:
THE GOOD OF WEEPING

Have you ever said or heard someone say the following? "God was really good to me today!" Or "God showed up in a huge way!" Or maybe even something like, "Wow, that was a "God" thing!" These exclamations are meant as expressions of praise and thankfulness to God. However, they are only reserved for what we consider joyous or what we would consider "good" things in our lives. I don't want anyone to stop praising God for these moments, but my question is, can we say the same thing when the opposite is true? Is God only present in the "good" things? Is God not around on "bad" days? Is Satan more powerful than God on certain days? The truth is that no matter what happens to us in this life, those statements are true. What you believe about what is good in your life will either sink you further into despair or lift you up out of the pit.

When hasn't God been good to you? When hasn't God shown up? What in the world is not a "God" thing? The problem is that we only define what is good by our definition of good. This is a problem because our definition of good is not good. God doesn't just do good things; he is good! The Psalmist says, *"You are good and do good; teach me your statutes."* *(Psalm 119:68)* Or, as I heard Tom Ascol preach once in a sermon, "God doesn't do things because they are good; things are good because God does them."[17] This will put a whole different perspective on your suffering and sorrow. We believe that God promises us that everything works out for our good. This promise is found in what Paul says to the Romans and is often misunderstood. *"And we know that for those who love God, all things work together for good, for those who are called according to his purpose." (Romans 8:28)* How many things work for good? All things!

Yes, but what does Paul mean by "all things?" Dan, but not everything that happened to me was good?! My question would be, according to whose standard are you judging those things as good or not? And this, my friends, is how you can begin to see weeping as a gift. Everything that happens to you works together for good according to the purposes of God. This includes physical ailments, suffering, "bad" days, "good" days, and all the in-between days. I believe that to credit God only with the so-called "good" things is to deny Scriptures such as:

"I form light and create darkness; I make well-being and create calamity; I am the Lord, who does all these things." (Isaiah

---

[17] A Tom Ascol sermon (circa 2012) from Grace Baptist Church, Cape Coral, Florida

45:7)

"The Lord has made everything for its purpose, even the wicked for the day of trouble." (Proverbs 16:4)

"Shall we receive good from God, and shall we not receive evil?" (Job 2:10)

"Who has spoken and it came to pass unless the Lord has commanded it? Is it not from the mouth of the Most High that good and bad come?" (Lamentations 3:37-38)

"For it has been granted to you that for your sake, you should not only believe but suffer." (Philippians 1:29)

This sentiment is felt in the Psalmist's words when he writes, *"The insolent smear me with lies, but with my whole heart I keep your precepts; their heart is unfeeling like fat, but I delight in your law. It is good for me that I was afflicted, that I might learn your statutes. The law of your mouth is better to me than thousands of gold and silver pieces." (Psalm 119:69-71)* The Psalmist was suffering great sorrow over people maligning him with lies. Affliction is not something that anyone wants to endure. However, during this time, the Psalmist acknowledged that *"it is good for me that I was afflicted."* How can that be true? How can our afflictions be good? It is because the psalmist knew what God was doing in him to create a greater dependence and trust that could only come through affliction. What was the purpose of this affliction for the psalmist? He says, *"that I might learn your statutes."* In other words, the psalmist was glad for the sorrows these enemies produced because they drove him to God. How different would we see our weeping if we could come to say, as the psalmist does, "It is good for me to be afflicted?"

Jonathan Edwards practiced this in his life and made it his mission. He didn't want to waste his afflictions and desired to praise God through them. So, he made it his resolve to see God in everything so that he could savor the goodness of God. Edwards wrote, "Resolved after afflictions to inquire what I am the better for them, what good I have got by them, and what I might have got by them."[18] I believe we would be well-served if we were to take an inventory of our afflictions and then examine them closely to see what "good" came out of it. If we fail to take inventory of our afflictions, we are wasting the lessons God wants us to learn through them. Instead of being driven to God's "statutes," we will be driven to the lies we tell ourselves, which are driven by our emotions. Our emotions have their source in our fallen natures and, therefore, cannot be trusted. The mantra of the world is to "trust your heart." However, God says that our hearts are not to be trusted. God told Jeremiah, *"The heart is deceitful above all things and desperately sick; who can*

---

[18] *https://www.monergism.com/resolutions-jonathan-edwards-1722-1723*

understand it." (Jeremiah 17:9) Suffice it to say that Jiminy Cricket did not know what he was talking about when he sang, "Let your conscience be your guide." Our conscience cannot be our guide without the guidance and instruction of the Holy Spirit.

Recently, we were saddened to learn that a good friend, Randy, was diagnosed with cancer. It took us all by surprise as a church, and we immediately began praying for him and his family. The treatment plan involved chemotherapy that was to last nearly six months before he'd be reevaluated. Others receiving this news would not take it well, as it would rock them spiritually, emotionally, and physically. Randy decided that he was not going to let cancer have the upper hand. He knew that this had entered his life by God's decree, and he would make the most of it. I remember he read a small booklet by John Piper, which was early in the process, entitled *Don't Waste Your Cancer*. Randy was determined early on to do precisely that and would not waste it. So, Randy used this new trial to be focused on God, read his word, and focus on his plan.

Randy also joined a leadership development group I began for men in our church. As a part of our group study and my effort to teach the men how to study and read the Word, we delved deep into James. The first few verses read: *"Count it all joy, my brothers, when you meet trials of various kinds, for you know that the testing of your faith produces steadfastness. And let steadfastness have its full effect, that you may be perfect and complete, lacking in nothing." (James 1:2-4)* As a commentary to what James says in verse 2 to *"count it all joy,"* Randy shared some words that encouraged our souls. Randy said about his cancer, "This is the best thing that has happened to me." He shared how God had already grown and stretched his faith and was growing him closer to Christ. In that booklet, John Piper wrote about his cancer journey and how he wasn't going to "waste" it. Piper saw the goodness of God in his cancer by saying, "The aim of God in our cancer (among a thousand other good things) is to knock props out from under our hearts so that we rely utterly on him."[19] Randy's testimony echoes the Psalmist's statement in Psalm 119:71. *"It is good for me that I was afflicted, that I might learn your statutes."* Yes, even in cancer, God is good. Cancer by itself is not good. God's using cancer in our lives is good. I'm sure Randy and his family have gone through sorrow over the last few months. However, those tears serve the purposes of God for their good. At the time of this writing, his cancer has stopped growing and has shrunk some. We praise God for these results and all God has done thus far.

I'm sure many reading this book would never consider how God could use cancer for his glory.

---

[19] *https://www.desiringgod.org/articles/dont-waste-your-cancer*

Perhaps you have cancer or know of someone dear to you who is suffering or has passed from this disease. No matter what cancer may do to us in this life, it won't have the last word. Even though you may weep now through your pain, know that one day, cancer and every other disease in human history will be gone forever. Christian, if God allows cancer in your life, just know that somehow it will be for your good. Don't take my word for it; trust what God has said in his Word.

I completely understand if you can't see the goodness of your tears. You may not see it today, tomorrow, or before your life ends. Sometimes, we don't get the answers we are seeking. We don't know why certain things happen to certain people and not to others. C.S. Lewis once wrote a book entitled *A Grief Observed*. It is a candid account of how he dealt with grief after the death of his wife. It reads almost like a journal at times but is a very helpful memoir on how grief is observed. Lewis said something in there that made me connect with the thoughts of failing to see the goodness of God. Lewis writes, "You can't see anything properly while your eyes are blurred with tears."[20] How true that has been in my life. If you fail to see God's goodness in any affliction, then realize that the tears meant for your good could hinder you.

---

[20] *Lewis, C.S, A Grief Observed, Harper Collins, New York, New York, 1994, pg. 45*

Take the time to wipe them away, focus on God, and then reevaluate your affliction.

God doesn't lie; all things work together for good. Our natural response is to want answers and want them now. However, getting the answers to your desired questions is challenging when your vision is blurred. Sorrow will play nasty tricks on your mind if you let it. Sometimes, we must be content to let the tears flow while trusting God in the unknown. If you try to look for answers, your perception of reality or truth might be twisted by your pain and grief. Trust in God and the knowledge that if you are in Christ, nothing in your life isn't good, and it is accomplishing his purpose for your life. Nobody is promised an easy life. Nobody is promised answers. Even though we think we deserve them, we don't. God doesn't owe us anything but wrath; if we get anything, it's all by grace.

Thomas Brooks says this of God's "owing" us an explanation of our affliction. "Shall we bind God to give us a reason of His doings, who is King of kings and Lord of lords and whose will is the true reason and only rule of justice? If the general grounds and reasons that God hath laid down in His Word, why He afflicts His people— namely, for their profit (Heb. 12:10); for the purging away of their sins (Isa, 1:25); for the reforming of their lives (Ps. 119:67,71); and for the saving of their souls (1 Cor. 11:32) — should work them to be silent and satisfied under all their afflictions; though God should never satisfy their curiosity in giving them an account of some more hidden causes which may lie secret in the abyss of His eternal knowledge and infallible will."[21]

Lewis learned this when he was deep in the pit of despair. He was looking for answers and couldn't "hear" God. However, once he realized his tears were blurring his vision, Lewis wrote, "I have gradually been coming to feel that the door is no longer shut and bolted. Was it my own frantic need that slammed it in my face? The time when there is nothing at all in your soul except a cry for help may be just the time when God can't give it: you are like the drowning man who can't be helped because he clutches and grabs. Perhaps your own reiterated cries deafen you to the voice you hoped to hear."[22] In other words, when you feel like nobody is coming to help you or that God is distant, perhaps they are not. Perhaps grief has gripped your heart so much that you are like a drowning man that people are trying to rescue but can't because of the resistance that grief is causing in your heart.

---

[21] *Smith, Dale W, Ore from the Puritans' Mine, Reformation Heritage Books, Grand Rapids, MI) 2020, pg. 9-10*

[22] *Lewis, C.S, A Grief Observed, Harper Collins, New York, New York, 1994, 46*

The thing about weeping is that it helps us realize that we are not strong enough to fight alone. Expressing sorrow is good for us because it allows us to admit through our tears that we need God. Spurgeon once preached, "We are different, each of us, but I am sure there is one thing in which we are all brought to unite in times of deep sorrow, namely, in a sense of helplessness."[23] Feeling helpless is the last place most of us want to be. Losing all sorts of control of your life is a scary place to be. However, were you ever really in control of your life? Were you powerful when you thought you were strong? Perhaps you were just relishing God's gifts as your strength? This is a hard lesson that Paul had to learn in his life. God gave Paul a thorn in the flesh to keep him from being conceited. Paul called this "thorn in the flesh" a "messenger of Satan" to harass him. We will not take the time here to speculate on the nature of his thorn. We can see from the text that Paul felt weakness because of this thorn. However, the lesson that the Lord taught him was important to what Paul considered his strength.

The Lord said to Paul, *"My grace is sufficient for you, for my power is made perfect in weakness." Therefore I will*

---

[23] *Charles Spurgeon, "The Exaltation of Christ," Sermon 101, NPSP (November 2, 1856). Http://www.spurgeon.org/sermons0101.htm*

boast all the more gladly of my weaknesses, so that the power of Christ may rest upon me. For the sake of Christ, then, I am content with weaknesses, insults, hardships, persecutions, and calamities. For when I am weak, then I am strong." (2 Corinthians 12:8–10)

How can we be strong when we are weak? It is because we understand that we must rely on God's sufficient grace. The "thorn in the flesh" was not a punishment from God to Paul. Instead, it was meant to be God's grace in his life to prevent him from becoming conceited. The thorn served a purpose in his life and was not for nothing. Through this experience, Paul understood that God's goodness is not solely found in deliverance from the thorn but also in the thorn itself. The thorn was good because it kept Paul dependent on the Lord.

No matter the severity of our pain, the only place to find solace is in the goodness of God during our sorrow. We must ground ourselves in this doctrine if our devotion will show itself to be a help. Finding peace and rest in ourselves or our solutions is tempting. However, the only thing that will nourish our souls at the end of the day is knowing that God is good no matter what. This world may promise us peace and security, but it can never deliver on its promises. Trust the God who not only does good but is good. I'm reminded of the old hymn by the Scottish pastor

Horatius Bonar called *I Heard the Voice of Jesus Say*. It is based on what Jesus said in Matthew 11:28-30. *"Come to me, all who labor and are heavy laden, and I will give you rest. Take my yoke upon you, and learn from me, for I am gentle and lowly in heart, and you will find rest for your souls. For my yoke is easy, and my burden is light."* Bonar writes,

> "I heard the voice of Jesus say,
> 'Come unto Me and rest;
> Lay down, thou weary one,
> lay down Thy head upon My breast.'
> I came to Jesus as I was,
> Weary and worn and sad;
> I found in Him a resting place,
> And He has made me glad."[24]

Friends, I don't know what is causing you sorrow right now, but this is good counsel. Rest in the goodness of God as found in Jesus Christ. I can promise you that, in Christ, God is good through it all. You may not want to define this sorrow as good, but what will the results be? This kind of goodness can only be seen through weak eyes. Even though you find it impossible to be thankful for your sorrows now, do your best to have that as your goal. Spurgeon says, "Be thankful for the providence which has made you poor, or sick, or sad; for by all this, Jesus works the life of

---

[24] *https://hymnary.org/hymn/LUYH2013/665*

your spirit and turns you to Himself."[25] These are not things that we usually think we ought to give thanks for. However, if we are to see God's goodness in our weeping, then it is a necessity.

> Although you feel as if your pain will never end,
> Let me give you some assurance, my friend,
> The Lion of the Tribe of Judah has won the war,
> And for this reason, you will one day weep no more.

---

[25] *Ritzema, Elliot, and Elizabeth Vince, eds. 2013. 300 Quotations for Preachers from the Modern Church. Pastorum Series. Bellingham, WA: Lexham Press.*

DISCUSSION QUESTIONS

1. How do you typically view suffering and sorrow in your life? Do you tend to see them as opportunities for growth and drawing closer to God, or do you struggle to find meaning and purpose in them?

2. The Psalmist in Psalm 119:71 says, "It is good for me that I was afflicted, that I might learn your statutes." How can we cultivate a mindset that sees affliction as an opportunity for spiritual growth and learning?

3. The chapter emphasized that our definition of "good" is not always aligned with God's definition of "good." How does this affect the way you view the circumstances and events in your life?

4. How does the concept of God's grace being sufficient for us in our weaknesses (2 Corinthians 12:8–10) impact your understanding of suffering and sorrow?

5. The chapter highlights the importance of taking an inventory of our afflictions and examining them closely to see what good came out of them. Have you ever done this in your own life? What did you discover? Why not begin today?

CHAPTER 4:
THE JOURNEY OF WEEPING

Since tears are a gift from God, what reward have your tears brought you? Or I can word it like this: To which destination are your tears leading you to? How are you using these tears to your advantage? Even if you don't realize it, your tears are doing something in you, and how you handle them determines where you will go. I understand that expressing sorrow is not a one-size-fits-all. Everyone processes grief differently, and we must not judge someone for still feeling sad. We can't predict how long someone's grief will last or if they will ever fully heal. Some people move through grief quickly, while others take their time. Some people do experience breakdowns along the way. It's important to remember that tears are a part of the journey, but they will lead you somewhere. The speed at which you arrive at your destination is up to you, but knowing where you're headed is important. Our tears can lead us to three destinations through our sorrows. Each of them is a different response to our pain. You have likely experienced all three responses, and perhaps all of them happened in the same week. A biblical example of this is found in the life of Job.

Job is a profound account of a man God blessed and loved. Here is God's testimony about Job: *"And the LORD said to Satan, 'Have you considered my servant Job, that there is none like him on the earth, a blameless and upright man, who fears God and turns away from evil?"(Job 1:8)* Job was a very blessed man. He had a big family, many animals, servants, and possessions. However, by God's ordinance, everything, including his health, was taken away in an instant. How would this man who loved God respond? I am grateful for Job's story because it shows us the journey of our tears. Let's examine and learn from the account of Job.

First, our tears can help draw us closer to God so we can learn to trust him through our sorrow. In this case, our tears are both a gift to express emotion and serve a sanctifying purpose, propelling us to worship God. Yes, this is the primary way that tears are a gift from God. They should propel us forward in our dependence on God. For example, Job responded with worship when he learned of the devastating losses. Worship? Yes, Job loved God so much and realized that his blessings were indeed a gift and were undeserved, so he thanked God in his sorrow. *"Then Job arose, tore his robe, shaved his head, fell on the ground, and worshiped. And he said, 'Naked I came from my mother's womb, and naked shall I return. The LORD gave, and the LORD has taken away; blessed be the name of the LORD.' In all this, Job did not sin or charge God with wrong." (Job 1:20-22)*

When Job worshipped God in his sorrow, it's not as if he was joyful that these things happened. Job mourned the loss of his family and possessions by tearing his robe, shaving his head, and falling on the ground. Here, we see in this account that it is possible to sorrow and to mourn in a good and godly way. Although Job was devastated and truly mourning, he used his tears to draw closer to God. Everything that Job had had come from God. He proclaimed, *"The Lord gave..."* but he also knew that when he lost it all, it was also by the hand of God. From a human perspective, Job had every right to be angry at God. He, in this moment, could have felt sorry for himself. Instead, he praised God in the most challenging moment of his life. He focused on God's goodness, God's sovereignty, and God's grace. When we weep, we can have a pity party for ourselves, or we can remember the One who is worthy to be praised. Again, it's not that Job wasn't sad! It was that Job used his sadness as a way to worship. Job knew it was not enough to praise God when things were good; we must also worship him in the darkest days of our lives.

The Psalmist in Psalm 42 had a similar experience. *"My tears have been my food day and night, while they say to me all the day long, 'Where is your God?'... Why are you cast down, O my soul, and why are you in turmoil within me? Hope in God; for I shall again praise him, my salvation and my God. My soul is cast down within me; therefore, I remember you from the land of Jordan and of Hermon, from Mount Mizar." (Psalm 42:3–6)*

Notice what the Psalmist does here as he sorrows. His sorrow was so deep that he could not even eat. What does the Psalmist do here? He uses his tears as a way to draw closer to God by remembering the goodness of God. He also preaches to himself (which I highly recommend doing) and reminds his soul from where his true help and salvation come. He then remembers God from a far and distant land. He truthfully and rightfully expresses raw emotion. He is so sad and down, but despite the depths of his sorrow, he uses his tears as worship. I know what you are thinking right now. Wow, Dan, yes, wouldn't it be nice to worship my way out of this pain? I get it, and yes, I've been there as well.

Worship isn't the only response we can give in our sorrow. Sometimes, we are so overcome by a situation that we cry until we can't cry anymore. After doing this and not thinking of our tears as worship, our tears can lead us to apathy. This state of apathy even serves to desensitize us to our sorrows and to any joy we might experience. This grief happens when we see our sorrows as more significant than life. Job also had this experience. Job? Do you mean the guy who worshipped when he lost everything? Yes, that guy. You see, one of the reasons that I love this story so much is that it's genuine. Job didn't stay up on that mountaintop of worshipping through his sorrow. He eventually lost his health and was inflicted by boils, and then everything changed.

After being inflicted with great pain from the boils, he was visited by three friends. Job was so distressed and sorrowful that he couldn't even speak. He was overcome by emotion, but instead of focusing on God, he focused on himself. *"And they sat with him on the ground seven days and seven nights, and no one spoke a word to him, for they saw that his suffering was very great." (Job 2:13)* Silence can sometimes be good. Sometimes we want to lie there and not say a word to anyone, and perhaps that could be a proper way to express our sorrow, but only briefly. For the longer we go in that state, our ability to worship God in pain will only grow more complex over time. Job essentially became paralyzed with sorrow, and not only could he not speak with his friends, but he also couldn't speak with God. Again, the only difference here is what Job did with his sorrows. His problem was not his grief; his problem was his inaction on his grief to worship God in this situation. You may say, "Give the guy a break; he lost everything and has no health left." The reason I speak with such bluntness on this issue is that if we wrongly use our tears and reject God in our sorrow, then we will only hurt ourselves. This is precisely the consequence that Job experienced.

Thirdly, our tears may also serve as a vehicle to drive us towards bitterness and anger. When we fail to worship God and trust him in all of his provisions, our hurt will only translate outwardly to hurting others mentally, emotionally, verbally, or perhaps even physically. Our tears can be used as a vehicle to drive us further from God if we believe the lies associated with them. In this way, our tears become enemies as they remind us of our pain. Our tears then become shackles in that we are enslaved to them instead of being set free by them. After sitting silently on the ground drowning in his sorrows, Job arose a different person. This was not the man *"who fears God and turns away from evil."* This was not the man who stood up against his wife when she told him to *"curse God and die"* (Job 2:9) and instead said, *"shall we not receive good from God, and shall we not receive evil?" (Job 2:10)* No, this was a different Job. It says he *"opened his mouth and cursed the day of his birth."* Job didn't even want to live any longer. He wished he would have died on the day he was born. He said, *"Why did I not die at birth, come out from the womb, and expire?" (Job 3:1)* When we give license to our tears, then what God gave as a gift can be used to hurt or harm others. In just a brief period, Job experienced significant loss and showed us how our weeping can be used against us.

Job's silence and refusal to worship God in pain made him bitter. This led him to complain much about

God. It led to demanding things from God that Job thought he deserved. What is ironic is that when this calamity first falls upon him, Job has sound doctrine. He knows that to receive good from the Lord, he must face difficult times. However, if we let them, our tears will drown out the truth we once believed. We will begin to see our trial only with bitterness, not with providence. We will see God as unjust and cruel rather than as excellent and holy.

Job's tears led him to a destination, and it didn't take him long to go from worship to driving into a ditch and wrecking his faith. Just as one drives down the highway on a long journey, we must also see ourselves. We must keep our eyes on the road and the destination. If we lose focus even for a second, we may not see the dangers on the road, which could cause our faith in God to be a casualty. Job's sin was not that he was displeased but the manner in which he handled his displeasure. Or as John Flavel writes, "There is no sin in complaining to God, but much wickedness in complaining of him. Griefs are eased by groans and heart pressures relieved by utterance."[26] Yes, the way we relieve the pressures of our grief is to give them to God. We cannot keep our emotions bottled up inside forever while ignoring everyone around us. Instead, we should give them to God in prayer. Additionally, we

---

[26] *Flavel, John, Facing Grief, The Banner of Truth Trust, Carlisle, PA, 2017, pg 16*

should rely on the support and guidance of our godly friends and elders, who can help us stay on the path towards God, rather than on the path away from Him.

What is the proper destination that God has for our tears? Is it so that God can learn something new about us? Is that what the test is? No, for God is omniscient and already knows all there is to know about us. He knew every decision we would make before time even began. Then what is the point of our weeping? Lewis gives us this insight, "God has not been trying an experiment on my faith or love in order to find out their quality. He knew it already. It was I who didn't. In this trial, He makes us occupy the dock, the witness box, and the bench all at once. He always knew that my temple was a house of cards. His only way of making me realize the fact was to knock it down."[27] Our sorrows and pain can be good because they remind us that we are not God. They can bring us to a point where we realize we can't go anywhere but to God. Our weeping is a gift that helps us journey on in life to learn to trust God above all.

I'll never forget the day I accidentally stumbled upon the hospital announcement of my birth. I was fourteen years old and looking for my *Nintendo Power*

---

[27] *Lewis, C.S, A Grief Observed, Harper Collins, New York, New York, 1994, pg. 52*

magazine in my parent's room. I found the paper from the hospital that announced my birth (a souvenir for my parents) but noticed something strange. The place that listed my father's name was blacked out with a permanent marker. With great curiosity, I went to ask my mother why she had blacked out my father's name. She told me with a sad tone to wait until my father returned home from work. When my father returned home, he told me the painful story that he was not my biological father. I was confused as he was the only father I had ever known. He was there when I was born and had given me his name. I shared this story in greater detail in my book *Grace Upon Grace*. However, the abbreviated version was that my biological father was a drunk who beat up my mother when he learned she was pregnant. He didn't want to be a father and attempted to cause a miscarriage. He was arrested and was never heard of or seen again. The only father I ever knew came as a knight in shining armor to rescue my mother. He took me in as his son, and the rest was history. It's a wonderful story of God's grace and mercy that reminds me so much of the gospel.

However, I share it here because this truth was painful for me to learn. I struggled greatly over the fact that my biological father hurt my mother and tried to kill me. I cried a lot that day, and that was the reason my parents had kept it from me all those years. Over the next five years, I grew bitter and angry at a man I had never met. I hated him. I only knew his name but that was enough to send chills up my spine. In my pain, I became angry at my parents for not telling me the truth, and I hated my biological father. I instantly had many questions about my life, all driven by anger. As I continued to cry, I just became angrier and more bitter.

When I graduated high school in 1995, I went to Bible College to prepare for the ministry. I was studying for the pastorate with all this anger and hatred in my heart. However, everything changed during a chapel message one day. I don't remember who the speaker was or what his message was that day. However, all I remember is being under great conviction of holding such anger in my heart. Yes, my bitterness even grew into resentment toward God. Here, I was studying the Bible in Bible college and was bitter towards God. I became broken over my sin and repented of my anger and bitterness. I chose to forgive a man I had never met. To this day, I have no idea of what has happened to him.

All I know is that during those days of anger, if I had ever met him in person, I would have punched him in the face. However, as my tears transformed into repentance, my heart softened. My tears were taking me to a destination that led me to be angry and bitter toward God for my biological father's sin. Thankfully, by his grace, he granted me repentance, and my tears for him are now different.

So, let us return to the beginning of this chapter. Since tears are a gift from God, what reward have your tears brought you? Or I can word it like this: To what destination are your tears leading you? How are you using these tears to your advantage? Even if you don't realize it, your tears are doing something in you, and how you handle them determines where they lead you. Job did learn from his tears after a painful rebuke from the Lord in chapters 38-41.

In Job 42, we read, *Then Job answered the LORD and said: "I know that you can do all things, and that no purpose of yours can be thwarted. 'Who is this that hides counsel without knowledge?' Therefore I have uttered what I did not understand, things too wonderful for me, which I did not know. 'Hear, and I will speak; I will question you, and you make it known to me.' I had heard of you by the hearing of the ear, but now my eye sees you; therefore I despise myself, and repent in dust and ashes." (Job 42:1-6)* Job realized that God was God and that he was not. When complaining about God, Job realized he spoke words he didn't quite understand. His tears brought him to a destination that went from worship to anger but back to worship.

Friend, keep your eyes on the road before you drive into the ditch, distracted by the lies that your tears preach. So, where have your tears taken you? Are you closer to God? Have you been driven away? Have you grown apathetic to life and feel numb? Learn from Job, get back in the car, and look to God. He is good, although the journey has told you otherwise. The only way out of your sorrow is to keep going toward him and not away from him. It's a long and painful journey but a necessary one. The journey may not feel as if it's worth it now but trust me it is. God is doing something far greater in you than you could ever realize. The good news is that the journey will come to an end.

> Although you feel as if your pain will never end,
> Let me give you some assurance, my friend,
> The Lion of the Tribe of Judah has won the war,
> And for this reason, you will one day weep no more.

DISCUSSION QUESTIONS

1. Consider the different responses to sorrow outlined in the discussion (worship, apathy, bitterness). Which response resonates with you the most, and why? How can you ensure that your tears lead you toward worship and trust in God?

2. Think about a situation in your life where you struggled with forgiveness. How did your tears influence your ability to forgive, or did they lead you down a path of bitterness? What steps can you take to find healing and forgiveness in such situations?

3. Lament is a common theme in the Bible, where individuals express deep sorrow and grief to God. How can we incorporate the practice of lament into our prayer life and find healing through honest and raw expressions of emotion?

4. What direction are you headed in your sorrow? Are you close to driving off the road into a ditch and wrecking your faith? What do you need to change to get back in the right direction?

5. Reflect on a time when you experienced joy or hope during a season of sorrow. What helped you find joy, and how can we cultivate a sense of hope even in difficult circumstances?

CHAPTER 5:
ANXIETY AND WEEPING

We all have some fear that is rooted deep in our hearts. Fear isn't necessarily a bad thing; in fact, it can be good. The most beneficial fear is, of course, to "fear God." The Scriptures are filled with this command, which is how every person should live. Other kinds of fears come from wisdom and keep us from being careless. We should fear when we are driving our vehicles, knowing that a moment of inattentiveness can lead to our death or the death of others. It is this kind of fear that keeps us sober-minded and safe. However, this isn't the kind of fear that produces weeping.

All of us struggle with some unhealthy fear. This unhealthy fear then results in a period of stress and anxiety, which harms us physically, emotionally, and spiritually. I have never seen a time where more unhealthy fear was expressed than in 2020. These were, of course, the days during the COVID-19 pandemic. It was a time that seemingly came out of nowhere, and it was hard to know whom to believe. The news, government officials, and social media only multiplied feelings of stress and fear. In the name of preserving people's physical health, the emotional and spiritual health of the world was jeopardized. A Gallup poll concluded that 2020 officially became the most stressful year in recent history. The poll discovered that "nearly 190 million people experienced significantly higher stress in 2020 than in years past."[28] We will never forget those days of confusion, government overreach, and the fear of the unknown. It was a test for all of us, which weakened some and emboldened others. It was a time in which God strengthened my convictions and refined my ecclesiology and understanding of his Word. I wouldn't say I liked that time, but I would be a weaker pastor today without it.

I will admit that the whole thing suckerpunched me. I felt much anxiety, fear, and worry during those days. As a pastor of a church with many elderly people, I feared that many in my congregation would get sick or die. I was worried about the spiritual impact on my people and the consequences of isolation. What should we do with our weekly gathering? Whom do we believe with the current information? How do you shepherd people with various strong opinions on different sides of the issue? Many other pastors and I lost a lot of sleep during those days. I had much unhealthy fear in me that had to be rooted out by God through this trial. Although I believed God was sovereign, my anxiety and my emotions didn't always show it.

---

[28] *https://www.forbes.com/sites/jackkelly/2021/07/31/global-emotions-survey-shows-record-high-levels-of-people-feeling-stressed-sad-angry-and-worried/?sh=421e5feb6963*

God used those days to sanctify me and many others. Unfortunately, we pre-recorded the services for a few weeks, with only a handful of us gathering at the church building. We then moved to a "drive-in" service out in the parking lot, which was better than staring at a camera, but was still no comparison to hugging and loving on my church family. After a few Sundays, we returned inside and gathered in person. Things were still different, as we had two services and were approaching things cautiously, but it was better than not gathering at all. I knew I could not get through that first service without weeping. I didn't even make it past the announcements and welcome at the beginning. I had to pause and gather my composure to keep speaking. What I missed the most during those days was hearing my church family sing hymns and read the Word out loud. Those were good tears that morning, but tears nonetheless that resulted from much stress, fear, and anxiety. I'm sure many of you were as confused and conflicted as I was during those days and worried much. You are not alone.

The time of the pandemic is only one example in which we were crippled by fear and anxiety. There are many other examples that we could give in our lives. However, I am grateful for examples from the Scriptures as well. As Israel approached the Red Sea, they saw Pharaoh's army fast approaching them. They were at a dead end as the sea blocked their way forward. Moses wrote, *"...the people of Israel lifted up their eyes, and behold, the Egyptians were marching after them, and they feared greatly. And the people of Israel cried out to the LORD." (Exodus 14:10)* Ok, so yes, that would be a situation that would cause fear in people. The question is, where does this fear take them? Some feared what Pharaoh would do to them as a punishment for leaving. How did their crying sound? *"They said to Moses, 'Is it because there are no graves in Egypt that you have taken us away to die in the wilderness? What have you done to us in bringing us out of Egypt? Is not this what we said to you in Egypt: 'Leave us alone that we may serve the Egyptians'? For it would have been better for us to serve the Egyptians than to die in the wilderness." (Exodus 14:11-12)* Their weeping and fear caused them to be bitter and angry towards God. Instead of fearing God more than Pharaoh, they reacted by showing where their faith indeed rested. Despite that, God still promised to rescue and fight for his people.

Another example can be found in the Book of Esther. After Mordecai and the Jews learned of the plot to kill all Jews in Persia, Mordecai wept and expressed sorrow by putting on sackcloth and ashes. Mordecai shows raw emotion as he fears the destruction of his people by a wicked man. *"Mordecai tore his clothes and put on sackcloth and ashes, and went out into the midst of the city, and he cried out with a loud and bitter cry..." (Esther 4:1-3)* Again, God's people wept over stressful times and evil people. What produces this kind of sorrow other than fear? Is there any justice? Where is God? What will God do to rescue us? Mordecai was "weeping bitterly" over this news – not only Mordecai but the rest of the Jews as well. *"And in every province, wherever the king's command and his decree reached, there was great mourning among the Jews, with fasting and weeping and lamenting, and many of them lay in sackcloth and ashes." (Esther 4:3)*

Yet another example can be found in Numbers 14. After hearing the report from the spies, Israel *"raised a loud cry, and the people wept that night." (Numbers 14:1)* What was so bad about the report? Some spies gave bad reports, causing fear among the people. They told the people that the promised land was bigger, stronger, and ready to destroy them. They caused them to have significant doubt in God's promises and faithfulness. So as a result, the nation wept all night long. We know the outcome: those who doubted God did not enter the promised land, and only Joshua and Caleb were allowed to enter from that original Exodus generation. Here, the nation failed to remember the promises of God and instead trusted in the fearful spies. They chose to listen and cling to bad news instead of the good word God had given to his servant Moses when he led them out of Egypt.

In all of these cases, the cause of fear is the same. When we fail to believe in God and trust him, we cause ourselves unnecessary stress and anxiety. The truth we must face is this: What if our worst fears are realized? What if everyone in my church had died from COVID? What if Pharaoh had gained ground and brought Israel back to Egypt? What if God had allowed Haman's plot to be successful? What if the giants of the land of Canaan had made it more difficult for Israel to advance? Would any of those things have changed God's promises? Has God promised us an easy life? What if everything was stripped away from us today? Would that change God's faithfulness? Does God owe us anything? What if we lose our jobs, health, families, and church? Does God not know these things? Much of our fear and anxiety can be eased by reminding ourselves of the truth. We may not want certain things to happen, but at the same time, we must not think we are owed anything—for we are not. The reality is that we are owed nothing but wrath, which makes grace all the sweeter.

Has stress or fear led to sleepless nights filled with tears for you? It has for me, and there's one time that I'll never forget. In 2008, our family moved to Florida from Pennsylvania to plant a new house church network. Although that sounds praiseworthy, it wasn't. It was more of an excuse to leave Pennsylvania because of a situation that angered me. I was full of pride and immaturity. After a short time in Florida, I realized how foolish it was to move away hastily. Providentially, it was at that same time that the economy collapsed, which made providing for my family complex. My decision to change "careers" and move away from full-time vocational ministry came at a most inconvenient time. The plan was to work a full-time secular job, but with the national recession spiraling, it became difficult to find a well-paying job. As the situation worsened, I became overwhelmed, discouraged, and distraught. It felt as if God was distant from me and quite angry with me. The crazy thing was that I had been a pastor for ten years and had told many to "trust the Lord," but I soon realized that I had no idea of what that meant.

One night, as my wife was sound asleep, I awoke in the middle of the night to a heaviness in my soul. A flood of emotions overtook me as I dealt with many insecurities, a deepening financial hole, and a dark spiritual battle. It was my fault. I had put my family in this situation because I was immature. I didn't know what else to do, so I prayed. As I prayed, I became even more uncomfortable. Isn't prayer supposed to help? Lying in bed wasn't working, so I decided to kneel. I carefully inched myself off the bed to avoid disturbing my wife. The last thing I wanted was for her to wake up and have to worry with me. Providing for the family was my burden to carry, not hers. As my knees hit the ground, tears flooded my eyes. What would I ask God for now that I hadn't already asked Him? What would I tell God now that He didn't already know? I was physically, mentally, and spiritually exhausted. However, even though I was on the floor, I wasn't even praying. I couldn't. I'm unsure how long I stayed on the floor like this, but it was a long time. When I finally got up, I said, "God, I need you." That was it. That was all I could muster. After all that time on the floor, at a loss for words, all I could say was, "God, I need you." I felt like such a failure.

Have you ever had a sleepless, teary night like that? What are you to do? Do what I tried to do but couldn't muster the strength or energy to do, pray. Puritan pastor William Perkins encourages us to pray in this way. He writes, "Let thine heart and tongue be still employed in prayer to the Lord: first, for patience in thy trouble; secondly, for comfort in thine affliction; thirdly, for strength in His mercy; fourthly, for deliverance at His pleasure. Yea, endeavor even to die praying when thou art in the depth of miseries; and at the gates of death there is a depth of God's mercy which is ready to hear and help thee."[29]

If you've had a night like that, know that you are not alone. Many have tossed and turned and worn themselves out with their tears. For example, even the mighty warrior King David cried multiple times at night. In Psalm 6, David had a sleepless night as he

---

[29] *Smith, Dale W, Ore from the Puritans' Mine, Reformation Heritage Books, Grand Rapids, MI) 2020, pg. 117*

feared. David wrote, *"I am weary with my moaning; every night I flood my bed with tears; I drench my couch with my weeping. My eye wastes away because of grief; it grows weak because of all my foes." (Psalm 6:6-7)* David's words describe a sad time in his life. David's bed was "drenched with tears and weeping." We don't know all the events that led up to these long nights for David. How did David deal with it? He flooded the bed with tears and wearied his eyes from the constant crying. That doesn't seem very manly. Or does it? Yes, David, the one whom God used to slay Goliath, the one who once collected double the amount of required Philistine foreskins, the one who wrestled with bears and lions, cried. There is nothing more manly than crying to the Lord in complete dependence.

Friends, God is still good if the worst possible thing happens to us today. Can I also say something here that needs to be said? Most of my "fears" never come to fruition. I worried about things that never happened and caused me a significant lack of sleep, productivity, and mental health. How much more would my time benefit from redirecting that energy to humbling myself to know the truth and marinate in it? We also act as if this life is all we have. No matter what you fear, it won't last forever. If you didn't know God, and this life was all you had, I guess there'd be much to fear. Soon, we will be in a place where all we have lost will fail compared to all we have gained. So, let us handle our stress and fear as David did in Psalm 18. *"In my distress, I called upon the Lord; to my God, I cried for help. From his temple, he heard my voice, and my cry to him reached his ears." (Psalm 18:6)*

Even though at that moment I felt helpless, my tears were producing in me that night a strength that would carry me many days ahead. Were my problems resolved that night? No, they were far from over. However, that sleepless night was for my good as God put me in a position where I had to really trust Him. We despise these sleepless nights in which our brains will not shut off. I hope that we never have to have one of those nights again, but I know we will. Your sleepless nights may not end with a resolution as you seek God in prayer. However, God works throughout the night, each night, through your tears producing in you a weight of glory. Don't lose heart, if you are even further down the hole, when the morning comes, than you were when you began. These tears serve a purpose that will be fulfilled either in this life or in the future. Let it be enough that he has heard you. Rest in the grand assurance of his sovereignty and promise to make everything new. The Lord is our Rock and Redeemer for those long, stress-filled nights we toss and turn. On these nights, I am always encouraged by the second verse of the hymn, *O Lord, my Rock and my Redeemer* which says:

"O Lord, my Rock and my Redeemer
Strong defender of my weary heart
My sword to fight the cruel deceiver
And my shield against his hateful darts
My song when enemies surround me
My hope when tides of sorrow rise
My joy when trials are abounding
Your faithfulness, my refuge in the night"[30]

One day, all your fears and stresses will vanish, and you will never fear or worry about anything earthly again. One day, you will not have to drench your pillow with your salty drops of sorrow. Ah, yes, no more sleepless nights filled with tears. No more stress, anxiety, or fear will ever be yours again. Please, sign me up for that!

Although you feel as if your pain will never end,
Let me give you some assurance, my friend,
The Lion of the Tribe of Judah has won the war,
And for this reason, you will one day weep no more.

---

[30] *Words by Nathan Stiff © 2017 Sovereign Grace Worship/ASCAP (adm. by Integrity Music) Sovereign Grace Music, a division of Sovereign Grace Churches. All rights reserved.*

DISCUSSION QUESTIONS

1. In what ways do you see unhealthy fear manifesting in your life or the lives of those around you?

2. How do you think fear impacts our ability to trust God's plan for our lives? How can we work towards overcoming this barrier? What can we learn from the Psalmist?

3. I shared some examples of fear in my life over the years and how God used that to grow me. What examples can you reflect on in your life? How did God use times of fear to grow you in your faith journey?

4. How often do you toss and turn at night because of fear and anxiety? What do you do to redirect that fear for your own good? How do you resonate with the Psalmist crying all night?

5. How much time do you waste worrying about things that never materialize? What can you do to change that? How can you change your thinking in order to trust God more?

CHAPTER 6:
FAILURE AND WEEPING

I hate to disappoint people. I know I can't make everyone happy, and trust me, I've tried. However, knowing that I have disappointed others, intentionally or not, eats at me. It is certainly something that I have had to deal with and address. As frustrating as that is, I can't control how others feel, nor can I convince some people of the truth. People will always believe and hear what they want to hear, and there isn't anything I can do about it. We can all share stories of regret and disappointment that have haunted us over the years. This regret may even bring upon oneself a great sadness, which leads to many tears. Even after those we have offended forgive us, we can find it almost impossible to forgive ourselves, and the pain has a lifetime's effect on every part of our being.

We can point to many examples of failure that are in the Scriptures. However, I most often think of the Apostle Peter. Peter is famously known as the eccentric, outgoing, stick-his-foot-in-his-mouth disciple of Jesus. Peter was frequently quick to speak before he realized what he had uttered. Remember when Jesus explained to the disciples that he had to suffer and die? Peter couldn't stand what Jesus was saying. Instead of listening to his Master and submitting to his teaching, he rebuked Jesus. *"Far be it from you, Lord! This shall never happen to you." (Matthew 16:22)* Peter spoke as if he were Satan, so Jesus issued a scathing rebuke. *"But he turned and said to Peter, 'Get behind me, Satan! You are a hindrance to me. For you are not setting your mind on the things of God, but on the things of man." (Matthew 16:23)* We can sort of understand where Peter was coming from when he made this statement. He loved the Lord. Jesus was his friend and Master. Peter would protect him and not let any harm come his way! Peter shows us that we can fail even when we try to do what we believe is right. How can we fail when we believe we are doing the right thing? It is because we think we know more than God does. Therefore, the right "motives" become wrong when fleshed out. Another example of Peter's doing the right thing the wrong way is when he attempted to walk on water with Jesus. Peter got out of the boat (the right thing) but instantly became afraid and forgot about the Lord. So, Peter then began to sink as he took his eyes off Jesus (see Matthew 14:22-33).

We can also look to the night that Jesus was arrested to see more failure from Peter. Peter could not pray with the Lord and the other disciples and chose to sleep instead (see Matthew 26:38-41). Later that evening, Judas approached with those who would arrest the Lord. Peter was angry at what was happening. In anger, he drew his sword and cut off the ear of Malchus, the servant of the high priest (see John 18:10-11). Again, even when Peter seems to have been doing a "good" thing, protecting his Master, it becomes a failure. He did not heed the teaching of his Lord and failed to see what was happening as a necessity. He reacted very humanly, and Jesus rebuked him for his aggressiveness.

Peter's most famous failure also happened that night, which the Lord said would happen. Just as Jesus had predicted his death and resurrection, he also prophesied that all the disciples would leave him. Peter refused to believe Jesus' words about his turning away. Despite what the others would do, Peter was bold enough to profess his allegiance to Christ. He said, *"Even if all fall away on account of you, I never will." (Matthew 26:33*) Jesus swiftly rebukes Peter by detailing his future failure by saying, *"this very night, before the rooster crows, you will disown me three times" (Matthew 26:34)* Instead of listening to his Master, Peter, still emphatic with pride, declared, *"Even if I have to die with you, I will never disown you.' And all the other disciples said the same." (Matthew 26:35)*

Peter's problem in each instance was that he thought way too much of himself. Peter would have done well to heed Paul's admonition to the Corinthians. *"Therefore, let anyone who thinks that he stands take heed lest he fall." (1 Corinthians 10:12)* In each instance, he thought that he couldn't fail because of something within himself. This is what led to the dreaded evening in which Peter did indeed deny the Lord. After seeing the Lord arrested, Peter was confronted three times, asking if he was one of the Lord's disciples. *"Then he began to invoke a curse on himself and to swear, 'I do not know the man.' And immediately the rooster crowed." (Matthew 26:74–75)* Peter went from standing his ground to instant regret. All it took was the sound of a rooster's crow to invoke a very painful and vivid flashback. It was at this moment that Peter knew he had blown it. He had failed the Lord, and it cut his heart like a finely sharpened knife. When he heard the rooster, he *"remembered the saying of Jesus, 'Before the rooster crows, you will deny me three times. And he went out and wept bitterly."* Peter didn't waste any time getting out of that place before anyone else could recognize him. All he could do was weep. He didn't just weep; he wept bitterly. The Greek word used for "bitterly" implies agony.[31] Peter was not just a little bit upset; he was beside himself.

Have you been there? Have you ever messed up so badly that it cost you? Have you ever felt shame after being exposed? Have you tossed and turned at night wishing you could go back and do something differently? Welcome to the club. In a sense, we all have failures. It's just that some of our failures are

---

[31] Swanson, James. 1997. *In Dictionary of Biblical Languages with Semantic Domains: Greek (New Testament), electronic ed. Oak Harbor: Logos Research Systems, Inc.*

more noticeable than others. Perhaps your failures are only known by you, and you wonder what people would think if they were to find out. Possibly, these failures are public, and you bear the shame of your family or friends. It hurts. What should we do then? Are our failures the end of the road? Does God want us to wallow in self-pity for the rest of our lives? Are we to bear a scarlet letter as a reminder? There are some genuine consequences to our sins and failures. Although we are forgiven in Christ Jesus, this doesn't mean our scars or pain will be erased in this life. For some, it will take a lifetime of healing and trusting in Christ for their new identity to be known. Are we to be punished by tears that will never end? The answer is, of course, no.

The problem is that we are our own worst enemies. Or as John Flavel wrote, "Of all the creatures that God ever made (devils only excepted), man is the most able and apt to be his own tormentor."[32] We torment ourselves for our failings, which never serves us well. Yes, we ought to mourn for our failings, but then we must repent and trust Christ to forgive us, and then we must forgive ourselves. I love what Martin Luther said when Satan reminds him of his failures. "So when the devil throws your sins in your face and declares that you deserve death and hell, tell him this: 'I

---

[32] *Flavel, John, Facing Grief, The Banner of Truth Trust, Carlisle, PA, 2017, 28*

admit that I deserve death and hell, what of it? For I know One who suffered and made satisfaction on my behalf. His name is Jesus Christ, Son of God, and where He is there I shall be also!"[33]

What happened to Peter? We all know that Peter went on to be the Apostle Peter! Peter, who preached Christ in the book of Acts, healed the sick and was imprisoned for the name of Jesus. However, before Peter could have the courage to do all that, he had to talk with Jesus about what happened. Peter saw the risen Lord (although he lost the race to the tomb — thanks, John, for that information) and spent many days with him. However, on one of those days, Jesus appeared to Peter and the other disciples. Peter said he was going fishing, which he loved, and which was his trade. Jesus called from the seashore to the men after a long night produced no fish. After following the instructions from the Lord, they had more fish than they knew what to do with! Peter recognized that it was the Lord and swam to shore.

On the shore, he had breakfast with Jesus on the beach, and the Lord asked him three times, *"Do you love me?"* Peter again emphatically replied with his love for the Lord! However, Jesus says something

---

[33] Luther, Martin *Letters of Spiritual Counsel*, trans. and ed. Theodore G. Tappert (Vancouver, British Columbia: Regent College, 2003), 86–87

extraordinary to Peter. *"Truly, truly, I say to you, when you were young, you used to dress yourself and walk wherever you wanted, but when you are old, you will stretch out your hands, and another will dress you and carry you where you do not want to go." (John 21:18)* This is an unusual way to end the conversation about loving Jesus and feeding sheep and the like. However, John gives us the significance of the statement. *"This he said to show by what kind of death he was to glorify God. And after saying this, he said to him, 'Follow me." (John 21:19)*

So, Jesus encourages Peter with news of his death? Yes! Why is that so encouraging? Remember that Peter had promised to die for Jesus if he had to, but he didn't keep his promise. He instead denied him three times. Jesus assured Peter that although he had failed, he would fulfill that promise. Peter would not fail in the end. Peter would live to be an older man and would eventually be martyred for the Lord. What was Jesus saying to Peter? Weep no more, Peter. I love you, forgive you, and your life will not end in failure. He then encourages Peter to *"Follow me."* Or, in other words, come on, we've got work to do. Yes, that is very encouraging! The next time we see Peter, he preaches on the Day of Pentecost, and 3,000 people trust Christ as Savior. Peter's big mouth often got him into big trouble. However, the Holy Spirit would also use that mouth to draw people in faith and repentance to believe the gospel. Peter's failure and restoration are so encouraging to me!

In the previous chapter, I wrote about the stress that moving to Florida had on my family and me. That move began the five most difficult years of my life. I had already been in pastoral ministry for ten years before we moved to Florida. After settling into our new home, we began planting a home church. We invited many people to our home, but nobody came. It was just myself, my wife, and our three children. It was very discouraging, to say the least. I knew it would be difficult, but I had no idea how difficult. It was just the five of us for some time. We did have one couple come to join us, which was encouraging. However, after a few months, we decided to end the church as nobody else was coming. I felt like a failure. I despised attending pastor meetings and seeing all the other successful church planters and pastors. I was envious of their position and "success" and coveted what they had.

What had happened to me? I had moved from our growing church to Florida from Pennsylvania, only to fall flat on my face. So, I decided returning to full-time vocational ministry would be best. I needed to provide for my family, and all I knew how to do was be a pastor, so that's what I wanted to return to. However, something happened that I didn't anticipate — nobody wanted me. I sent resumes all over the country. I felt washed up, unusable, and had lost all confidence. As my family sank deeper into a financial hole, I began to wallow in failure. I had failed God by abruptly leaving Pennsylvania. I had abandoned God's people, whom I had been called to care for. I wouldn't have been in this predicament if I had not done that. Why had I been so stupid? What was wrong with me? I continued sending out resumes for the next four years, only to be rejected by everyone. Little did I know then, but it was exactly what God wanted for me. The Lord had to rip many idols out of my heart. I was a prideful man who idolized my identity in ministry. I soon came to realize that I had an identity crisis, an identity in Christ crisis, to be precise.

My identity had become what I did for Christ (serve as a pastor) and not in who I was in Christ (a Christian first and foremost). It hurt me when I could no longer have my idol (my title and the applause of people). I didn't know it then, but I now believe that I was experiencing the discipline of the Lord. It wasn't other churches that had rejected me from being their pastor; it was God. God knew I could not enter the ministry until my heart had been made right. It took five painful years to realize what I had missed. It was a humbling experience, and the Lord brought me to the place I needed to be — rock bottom.

At rock bottom, God had changed me forever. I reached a place where I was satisfied with God and not with what I did for God. I was content with never preaching again if that's what the Lord had for my life. This was because the Lord reformed everything about me. God changed my theology, ministry philosophy, and preaching during this humbling time. I was blessed by the influence of godly men such as Tom Ascol and Founders Ministries, who cared about me. It's a long story, but after I surrendered all my failures to God, the discipline process I was under ended. By God's providence, I became the pastor of Northwest Baptist Church in April 2013, and without my failure, I would never have been ready to pastor these dear people. I would have ruined them unless God had not ruined me first. Great is his faithfulness! This is why I resonate so much with Peter. Without that breakfast on the beach and being filled with the Holy Spirit, how does Peter preach in Acts 2 on the Day of Pentecost?

One of the greatest books ever written is *Pilgrim's Progress* by John Bunyan. This timeless work was written while Bunyan was imprisoned in England for being a non-conformist pastor. This book is an allegory of the Christian life. It is a book that all Christians should read and read again throughout their life. The story follows a man named "Christian" in his faith journey. He encounters many different experiences on this journey that are allegorical of the

Christian life. Christian is marching toward the "Celestial City" and he has been ordered to stay on the "King's Highway" in order to reach it. He doesn't always follow these instructions which gets him in all sorts of trouble. One of these troubling moments is relevant to our discussion in this chapter.

Despair is a common and real thing that humans experience. This state of being comes from the deepest and darkest places of our emotions. Especially the despair that comes with our own failures and shortcomings. On their journey, Christian and his friend Hopeful, are tempted to veer off the King's Highway for an easier road to reach the Celestial City. They soon encounter great danger as they proceed on this new path. This leads them to being captured by Giant Despair who then takes them to Doubting Castle. The Giant locks up the two friends in a cage and makes them suffer. Christian doesn't deal with this failure well. Bunyan writes, "Now in this place Christian had double sorrow, because it was through his unadvised haste that they were brought into this distress."[34] Perhaps you know a little more why I resonate so much with this story. It reminds me of my life, and if you are honest, it will remind you of yours. Because of my mistakes, I veered off the path and,

---

[34] *Bunyan, John, Pilgrim's Progress, Moody Bible Institute (Chicago, Il) 2007 edition, pg 151*

because of my circumstances, fell prey to "Giant Despair," who locked me up in a cage. The Giant tried everything in his power to discourage the two friends during their imprisonment. He even suggested that they take their own life. However, the brothers decided never to do such a thing no matter how bad it was in this captivity.

The irony in this story is that their decision led them there and kept them there. However, the power to be free was also readily available, although they had forgotten. Christian soon remembered that he had a key named "Promise." Christian said, "What a fool am I, to lie in a stinking dungeon, when I may as well walk at liberty! I have a key in my bosom called Promise, that will, I am persuaded, open any lock in Doubting Castle."[35] With this key, he unlocks his cage, and both friends escape as the Giant becomes immobile and unable to chase after them. The same is true for us. We also possess a promise that we can use to unlock the prisons that we confine ourselves to live in. The promise is the Word of God and the promises of God. Once the Pilgrims realized this truth, they were set free, and we can be as well. The promises of God are sufficient for our failures, stresses, and our weeping.

---

[35] *Bunyan, John, Pilgrim's Progress, Moody Bible Institute (Chicago, Il) 2007 edition, pg 157*

Friends, we have all failed the Lord in some way or another. Some of us have failed in very public ways, but we have all failed in private ways. However, we must not let those failures define us or keep us down. If Peter could rise and serve Christ faithfully, then so can we. Jesus didn't want Peter to wallow away in his miseries for the rest of his life. He had work for Peter to do, *"Feed my lambs."* There is a time for weeping, and Peter certainly did that, and it got him down. I understand that some failures will stick with us for the rest of our lives. However, I pray that you can see past them to the beautiful news of the gospel and meditate on God's love for us. If you can't get there, know that day is also coming for you. Although you and I have weeping induced by our failures, the Lord knows about them and still chooses us anyway. If he chose Peter despite his epic failures, we are also within his scope of usefulness. May we not focus on our failures but on his victory. We must learn and repent from our failures but never stay in them. We must be humbled and face some consequences in this life, but we must also keep our eyes on Christ.

Although we weep over our failures now, one day, that will be a thing of the past. My prayer is that no matter our failures, we will rest in the grace, mercy, and the gospel of Christ to handle our sorrow.

Although you feel as if your pain will never end,
Let me give you some assurance, my friend,
The Lion of the Tribe of Judah has won the war,
And for this reason, you will one day weep no more.

DISCUSSION QUESTIONS

1. How do you personally relate to the struggle of feeling like a failure or experiencing disappointment? Can you share a specific experience where this was particularly challenging for you?

2. What steps can you take to avoid placing your identity in failure? How can we cultivate a deeper, more authentic relationship with God that isn't dependent on external measures of success?

3. How does the concept of God's sovereignty and His ability to work all things together for good impact our understanding of failure and disappointment?

4. We all understand that we can't undo mistakes from our past. However, what can we do to ensure that our future isn't defined by our past failures?

5. I shared some failures in my life. How do they resonate with your experiences?

CHAPTER 7:
RELATIONSHIPS AND WEEPING

At the core of the human experience are relationships with other people. This need for connection is seen early in the Bible as Adam discovers that nobody else is like him. It didn't take Adam long to find out that he was alone and that there was *"no helper fit for him." (Genesis 2:20)* This, of course, is what God used to bring Adam's wife Eve to him by showing him his need for companionship. Why does Adam need companionship? Why is this a need for human beings? It is a need because it is how we were created by God. Adam was created perfectly, yet he had something missing and didn't even know it. Adam was created from the dust of the ground and made in God's image to reflect his Creator. God made Adam distinct from the rest of creation. God created the animals, but the animals are not made in God's image. God made the angels, but they are not image-bearers of God. Our souls reflect a little of who our Creator is in his being. So, who or what is God? God is a Trinity. He is one in his essence but three in his persons. We understand God somewhat by understanding him in his personhood. God is Father, Son, and Spirit. Therefore, we can say that God lives in a relationship with himself and has always been content and complete.

We desire relationships because we are made in God's image. This is the longing Adam felt in his soul when he realized he was different from anything God had made. We were not created to live in isolation apart from others. For introverts, some of your dream vacations are to escape alone in some remote cabin away from everyone. That may be ideal for a season, but you were created to be connected to others. We were not made to be alone or to live life alone. We certainly are facing an epidemic of loneliness in this world. Being severed from those we love has devastating effects on our whole being. Today, some parents are estranged from their children. Couples have divorced after years of marriage. Best friends won't speak or see each other anymore. Church members have left churches after some hurt or trauma. Often, there are siblings who end up despising each other, and the list goes on.

You have likely experienced some sort of broken relationship in your life. If you haven't, then you probably will at some point in the future. That is just the reality of our broken world. These relationships come crashing down for various reasons: greed, pride, abuse, anger, gossip, political differences, etc. The list stating the reasons for failed relationships can fill more pages than this book can hold. More than likely, at the heart of every broken relationship is sin. Sin is the marring of the image of God, so it should come as no surprise that when relationships go wrong, they hurt so much. When relationships are damaged, this destroys and robs us of what we crave from our Creator. We were made to love and live with others in community. So when those relationships are severed, it leaves an indelible impact upon our souls which causes much weeping.

One of the most famous examples of broken relationships in the Scriptures is the story of Joseph and his brothers. Joseph was the firstborn son of Jacob's favorite wife Rachel. Jacob had wanted to marry a woman named Rachel. However, Laban tricked Jacob into marrying Rachel's older sister, Leah. Jacob married Leah but had to work an additional seven years for Rachel's hand. Leah gave Jacob children, but Rachel was barren. So, when Rachel finally had a son, it was a big deal to Jacob, and that turmoil in his life would soon cause much chaos in his family.

Jacob's favoritism of Joseph was evident to the rest of his sons, which drove them to hate Joseph. *"Now Israel loved Joseph more than any of his sons because he was the son of his old age. And he made him a robe of many colors. But when his brothers saw that their father loved him more than all his brothers, they hated him and could not speak peacefully to him." (Genesis 37:3-4)* This hatred only continued to grow over time, and they couldn't even stand to listen to Joseph. The brothers eventually planned his death but later changed their minds and sold him as a slave and then lied to Jacob. They told their father that wild animals had torn Joseph apart and even brought home Joseph's coat, decorated with animal blood as proof. This led to a great mourning for Jacob as he thought his favored son was gone. *"Then Jacob tore his garments and put sackcloth on his loins and mourned for his son many days. All his sons and all his daughters rose to comfort him, but he refused to be comforted and said, 'No, I shall go down to Sheol to my son, mourning.' Thus, his father wept for him." (Genesis 37:34-35)*

Sin causes so much sorrow. First, it was Laban's sin that had tricked Jacob. Then, Jacob's favoritism of Joseph led to the brother's great sin. Can you imagine how Jacob felt? How many parents have wept over the sin that drove their families apart? How many families have wept because of the selfishness that caused relationships to be severed? We find Joseph in Egypt and second in command under Pharaoh when we fast forward years later. God had used him to save the world from famine by interpreting Pharaoh's dreams. As the world needed food, the brothers came to Egypt. Among those who came were Joseph's brothers. Joseph realized who they were and saw they had brought their youngest brother, Benjamin. Benjamin was his full brother having been born to his mother, Rachel. The sight of Benjamin was too much for Joseph to bear, and the tears began to pool in his eyes.

So, what did Joseph do? *"Then Joseph hurried out, for his compassion grew warm for his brother, and he sought a place to weep. And he entered his chamber and wept there." (Genesis 43:30)* Joseph wept. So much pain. So many tears. So much sin. Jacob's favoritism, the brothers' lies, and hatred led to much sorrow for an entire family. It led to Joseph losing years of his life with his family. It led to Jacob thinking that a wild animal had devoured one of his children.

When we are reminded of the pain that others have caused, we feel immense sorrow. These feelings can be fueled by resentment or anger. Joseph also wept for compassion as he looked at Benjamin. I wonder if, throughout the years, he often wondered what had become of his little brother. Did his other brothers get rid of Benjamin as they had done to him? Joseph was overcome with emotion, knowing that Benjamin was still well. He couldn't contain it, so he went to another room to hide his weeping. The rush of memories, the years of separation, and his love for his father were all hitting him at once. Why? Why did it matter to Joseph? This was his family! These people are his flesh and blood, and they had been severed from him. Joseph went to Egypt alone, not knowing a single soul but trusting God to protect him.

That was not the last time he would weep. After giving his brothers a difficult time, he wept over them as he told them the truth. Joseph didn't tell them the truth immediately, but he finally reached a point where he could no longer contain himself. *"Then Joseph could not control himself before all those who stood by him. He cried, 'Make everyone go out from me.' So no one stayed with him when Joseph made himself known to his brothers. And he wept aloud, so that the Egyptians heard it, and the household of Pharaoh heard it. And Joseph said to his brothers, "I am Joseph! Is my father still alive?" But his brothers could not answer him, for they were dismayed at his presence." (Genesis 45:1-3)* Joseph wept so loud that the Egyptians heard him weeping. He reveals the truth, and the first thing he wants to know is, "*Is my father still alive?*" Joseph had felt the pain of separation for years, and it was all coming out; Joseph's tears at this moment were natural and expected. However, don't forget that these tears are also a gift of God. After years of having these emotions bottled up, the waterworks began to flow in Egypt.

Despite that, God used his gift (tears) for their good. The brothers were terrified that Joseph was going to seek revenge on them. However, that was not what Joseph was thinking at all. Instead, through his tears, God had healed him by showing him the goodness of God. Joseph said, *"Do not fear, for am I in the place of God? As for you, you meant evil against me, but God meant it for good, to bring it about that many people should be kept alive as they are today. So do not fear; I will provide for you and your little ones." Thus, he comforted them and spoke kindly to them." (Genesis 50:19-21)* Even though the brothers meant evil towards Joseph and Jacob, God meant all their evil for good. That's how God works in all our lives. Do we all get to have the ending that Joseph and his family did? No, that is not the happy ending that we all see in our sorrow. I wish that were true, but it's not. Sometimes, there is no reunion. Oftentimes, there is no repentance and reconciliation. I wish it didn't have to happen that way. However, we know that through something so tragic, God glorifies himself in ways we could never comprehend. God used the sin of these brothers not only to save Joseph's family but also to save the whole world.

There are many parallels between the life of Joseph and that of Jesus. Jesus was rejected by his brothers. *"He was in the world, and the world was made through him, yet the world did not know him. He came to his own, and his own people did not receive him." (John 1:10-11)* Jesus, who was God himself in human form, was rejected by and killed by his own nation, was thought of as crazy by his own immediate family (Mark 3:20-21), had many of his own followers give up on him (John 6:66), was betrayed by Judas, denied by Peter who was one in his inner circle, and then when it came down to the hour of the arrest, the disciples all scattered and left him. Mary had also blamed him for her own brother's death because Jesus hadn't been there to heal him (John 11:32). Jesus wept over the future destruction of Jerusalem (which happened in 70 AD) as he considered how the Jews had rejected him as their Messiah and did not know that it was he for whom they had been waiting (Luke 19:41-44).

One of the most painful broken relationships happens when a married couple divorces. It doesn't matter who was more at fault in the divorce; divorce leaves a fracturing of what God has joined together. This is why divorce hurts so badly. When you give yourself to someone in the covenant of marriage, you give them your heart, body, and mind. It is impossible to give yourself to someone else this way and not get hurt when a separation occurs. The Bible gives only two valid reasons for a divorce. These reasons are never to be considered as a "first option" but only when all other possibilities have been exhausted. These grounds are given in cases of "sexual immorality" (See Matthew 5:32, 19:9) and for abandonment by an unbeliever (1 Corinthians 7:15). As a pastor, I have had to counsel couples and have witnessed the scars and pain that divorce leaves behind in a family, a church, and a community. It is never easy, and it is never without pain. I've been around long enough to understand that it's never just one person's fault. Even if most of the blame can be placed on one person, the other spouse is usually not totally innocent.

A marriage is, after all, two sinners who have joined together in covenant. Wherever there are sinners, there will be problems. Some who have divorced can move on and live peaceful lives. Others are unable to do so, living with regret, emptiness, and pain while others reconcile or remarry. No matter your situation, know that your identity is not connected with your relationship status. You are not less of a person because you are divorced or single. You might want to find someone else to bring purpose, happiness, satisfaction, and fulfillment. You may think that those things are impossible without a spouse. Let me assure you that you don't need a spouse to find those things. God may grant that you remarry, but then again, he may not. Regardless of what the Lord desires for you, find your identity, joy, and purpose in him. Glorify God in your singleness now and be satisfied in him. Yes, I know, I write this as a married man who can't even imagine a day without my wife. This counsel I have given is easier to give than it is to be followed. What you desire is natural because of how your Creator has made you after his image. Seek relationships to fill that void (romantic or close friendships) in a God-honoring, Christ-exalting, biblically obedient manner.

There is no doubt some who are reading this right now and have memories flooding back of former spouses, friends, and relatives from whom you are estranged. I have experienced some of these broken relationships and know your pain. I'm sure that some of you are afraid to have any close relationships again because of the fear of being hurt again. You may have wept over these relationships but let me assure you that your tears are not for nothing. Use those tears to fuel your prayers for those relationships which have been severed from you. May your tears bring you to a place of healing, forgiveness, and restoration. There may not be perfect restoration in this life for all these relationships, but one day, all will be made right, and you won't always feel the way you do. As much as it is up to you, seek restoration. When sin is eradicated, all the brokenness will be gone. There will be nothing but peace in the new heavens and new earth and never a need to reconcile with anyone again. We will no longer hurt or weep for those broken relationships. That will be a glorious day.

> Although it seems as if your pain will never end,
> Let me give you some assurance, my friend,
> The Lion of the Tribe of Judah has won the war,
> And for this reason, you will one day weep no more.

DISCUSSION QUESTIONS

1. Reflecting on the story of Joseph and his brothers, how can we apply the principles of forgiveness and reconciliation to our own broken relationships? What steps can we take towards healing and restoration?

2. In the context of loneliness and isolation, how can we actively seek and cultivate meaningful relationships in our lives? What practical steps can we take to build community and connection?

3. Why do we long for companionship and friendship with others? Why does it hurt so bad when relationships go badly?

4. For those who have experienced divorce or broken marriages, how can we offer support and care as a church? How can we encourage individuals to find their identity and fulfillment in God, regardless of their relationship status?

5. How can we use our experiences of broken relationships and pain to empathize with others and offer hope and healing? How can our tears and sorrows be a means of drawing us closer to God and His purposes for our lives?

CHAPTER 8:
JUSTICE AND WEEPING

It would be a massive understatement to say there has been so much evil in this world. The sin that began in the garden continues to snowball throughout human history, leaving many victims in its wake. There have been massive crimes against humanity by humans. This is evident in the Bible and any honest history book you pick up. All we need to consider are the crimes of evil dictators such as Hitler, who, through his evil, massacred six million Jews. Or Stalin, who killed, imprisoned, and forced his people to work in labor camps and starve. There was Pol Pot, who was responsible for the genocide of 1.7 million people.

One that hits a little closer to home for me is Fidel Castro. Castro was the dictator of Cuba, and under his socialist policies, he killed, imprisoned, and sent the nation into poverty while he lived in luxury. My grandfather was once a political prisoner for opposing Castro which led to the government's confiscating his property – a farm near the beach. As a result, they were forced to live in the inner city. It was only by the grace and mercy of God that they managed to flee this great oppression legally. Without that great injustice, my life would have been much different. God is good even when evil men flaunt their wickedness. Nobody can thwart God's purposes for our lives. God will have the last word over Fidel Castro and all dictators who oppress people.

The most tragic of all injustices has been, of course, the slaughter of over 62 million babies since the passing of Roe vs. Wade in 1973. Recently, the Supreme Court has overturned that legal opinion, which has allowed certain states to ban abortion. However, some are trying to codify it into US law, which would make the slaughter legal everywhere in the United States. Regardless of the Supreme Court decision, the pre-born continue to be slaughtered in the womb. This nation is under God's judgment for such great wickedness and will continue to be unless we repent. May God have mercy upon us.

There has been much talk in the last few years about the word justice. We want to be careful how we use that word. The push from many once-solid evangelicals has been to discuss the need for social justice. Social justice is rooted in Marxist ideology, seeking "justice" by human standards of interpretation. It labels all who do not bow their knee to their standards of justice as hateful, racist, and misogynist. What one might consider just, another might feel as unjust. Social justice is relative to human culture or sensitivities. We assume God's role when we play those games and interpret justice through a human lens. We must ask, then, what is justice? How do we consider one thing to be just and another to be unjust? The answer, of course, is that no human being can determine standards of justice apart from a higher authority. Since justice is a legal word, we must consider what laws are being broken to consider an injustice. Human laws are not enough to define these things, as different cultures have different standards of justice. We must appeal to God since he is the Creator of everything and he himself is the Lawgiver. Injustice must be defined as breaking the law of God. In particular, we are speaking of God's moral law. The moral law is the designation that theologians have given to the second table of the Ten Commandments. The first four commandments deal with our relationship with God, while the remaining six deal with our relationship with one another. Therefore, any injustice must be defined as breaking God's law.

The push for social justice has happened in evangelical circles over the last decade or so. To be more compassionate, some evangelicals have adopted godless ideologies according to the standards of men. Critical Race Theory and Intersectionality are ideas birthed by Marxists, atheists, and others who oppose biblical truth. Racism is evil and must be repudiated. However, not any one person or people group gets to decide what is racist and what isn't. You see, the problem with dealing with the standards of men is simply this— it is never enough. The goalposts are always being moved until these activists get you to succumb to their woke and liberal agendas.

So, we must ask the question, does God care about injustice? Of course he does! However, when we want to care about what God cares about, we must define things God's way and not by the standards of men. For more on this topic, I encourage you to read Voddie Baucham's book *Fault Lines*, a good starting place to see what we are against. Our God certainly cares about oppression and injustices committed against his image bearers. For this, we only look to the Scriptures to see that God cares and how people who suffer can look to God alone for solace and comfort.

Justice is not isolated from God. In Isaiah, we read, *"For the Lord is a God of justice." (Isaiah 30:18)* The Bible speaks of true justice as being what God always does. For example, Moses writes, *"The Rock, his work is perfect, for all his ways are justice." (Deuteronomy 32:4)* Therefore, God can't be unjust! All his ways are just! Why? Because God loves his law, which reflects his character. Also, the Psalmist says, *"The King in his might loves justice."* (Psalm 99:4, see also Psalm 33:5, 37:28). In Isaiah, we also see God say, *"For I the Lord love justice; I hate robbery and wrong..." (Isaiah 61:8)*

Justice is not only who God is and what he loves but also what he requires. *"He has told you, O man, what is good; and what does the Lord require of you but to do justice, and to love kindness, and to walk humbly with your God." (Micah 6:18)* Conservative Christians who have opposed the social justice movement have been labeled as racist, misogynist, and haters of the poor and oppressed. However, is this true? It is only valid if you use the standards of men. We oppose such matters of social justice because these standards are not in accordance with God's law. So, do conservative Christians not care about justice?

The better question is not whether Christians should care about justice but how we define justice. As we saw from those Scriptures, true justice flows from God's law, nature, and person. Justice is caring for his image-bearers (humans) according to his law. This is why Jesus says the second greatest commandment is *"You shall love your neighbor as yourself" (Matthew 22:39),* which, of course, flows from the greatest commandment, which is *"You shall love the Lord your God with all your heart and with all your soul and with all your mind." (Matthew 22:37)* So yes, conservative Christians should care about justice for to stand for justice is to obey God's law.

We must understand that each sin is an injustice against our God. Therefore, each act of injustice, properly defined, is a sin. Each sin is an attempt to rob God of his glory and to claim it as our own. Therefore, the first great injustice committed by humans happened in the garden when Adam and Eve rebelled against God. Outside the garden, the first act of injustice happens when Cain kills his brother Abel. The Lord's conversation with Cain revealed how he felt about the taking of Abel's life. *And the Lord said, "What have you done? The voice of your brother's blood is crying to me from the ground." (Genesis 4:10)* Abel's blood was not literally crying out to God from the ground. This is symbolic language that shows us that Abel's murder was not hidden from God. God was aware of Cain's sin and told him that his brother's blood was crying out for justice. What law did Cain break that made this unjust? Cain broke the sixth commandment, which is *"You shall not murder." (Exodus 20:13)* Abel's blood cries out to God for justice because an unjust act against his law had been committed.

    I've known people close to me who have experienced someone being murdered in their family. Even I, had a good pastor friend murdered while he was walking up to his church office in 2014. It seems that every year, there is an ever-increasing rise in violent crimes and mass shootings. Certain cities, like Chicago, are out of control as the murder rate continues to increase. Murder is vile because it takes away the very precious gift of life itself. It mars the image of God in that person and causes death. Does God care? Yes, he does, and we can see that the blood of Abel crying out does not escape God's notice. People may get away with murder in this life, but they will not on Judgment Day. Every murderer will be held responsible before the Judge. No murder will be swept under the rug and forgotten about on Judgment Day. For those murderers who have repented of their sins and trusted in Christ alone, they are forgiven as their due punishment is given to Christ. For murderers who have repented of their sins and trusted in Christ to be saved, Christ has taken their place and their wrath on the cross.

Does God care about those who have suffered at the hands of racists? Does he consider those whom true oppressors have broken down? Yes, he certainly does! We see this clearly as God hears the oppression of the Jewish people in Egypt. After 400 years of being enslaved and mistreated, Moses wrote, *"During those many days the king of Egypt died, and the people of Israel groaned because of their slavery and cried out for help. Their cry for rescue from slavery came up to God." (Exodus 2:23)* The Israelites were given hard and unfair labor by their taskmasters. They were abused with harsh and unjust discipline. When they cried out for help, their cry came up to God. Did he care? Was God listening? Yes, he was, *"Then the Lord said, "I have surely seen the affliction of my people who are in Egypt and have heard their cry because of their taskmasters. I know their sufferings…and now, behold, the cry of the people of Israel has come to me, and I have also seen the oppression with which the Egyptians oppress them." (Exodus 3:7,9)* Yes, God sees, hears, and knows the oppression of his people. There will be justice for every person who has ever been mistreated and maligned as an image bearer of God. Those guilty of racism and partiality must have true repentance or face God's wrath. There will be justice for all those who were sinned against in these ways. The tears that many have shed over racism in this life have not escaped God's care or concern. God sees you and hears you.

Another form of injustice that has caused much weeping in this life is the sin of sexual abuse. Many have wept over sins against them in this way. Many suffer a lifetime of trauma, whether it be physical, emotional, or spiritual, because of perversions committed against them as children. There are untold numbers of children whom predators molested. This evil has happened in schools, relatives' homes, community groups, and churches. Some women have been raped by relatives, perverted men, strangers, and even trusted friends. Our sexuality is a precious gift of God, and when it is violated, it leaves scars that seem humanly impossible to overcome. As a pastor, I have done much counseling for people who were sexually abused either as children or adults. These wounds run deep and require many years of healing. The Bible contains many examples of sexual abuse. I am grateful for this so that those who have been abused might find solace and empathy from the Scriptures.

One of the most heartbreaking of these stories is found in 2 Samuel 13, when King David's son rapes his half-sister, Tamar. Not only was Amnon guilty of rape but also of incest. The evil plan was conceived when Amnon had an evil friend named Jonadab. He suggested that Amnon fake being sick so that Tamar would come to care for him. She came and cooked for him, and then he forced her to sleep with him. She said no, *"But he would not listen to her, and being stronger than she, he violated her and lay with her." (2 Samuel 13:14)* He raped his sister and robbed her of her virginity. This devastated Tamar and sent her into a state of deep weeping. *"And Tamar put ashes on her head and tore the long robe that she wore. And she laid her hand on her head and went away, crying aloud as she went." (2 Samuel 13:19)* There is another tragic example of sexual abuse and perversion in Judges 19-20. It's a grotesque and horrifying incident about a woman who is raped, abused, killed, and mutilated in the city of Gibeah. I find it the most challenging Bible passage to read and preach about. It reminds us of the horror of sexual abuse and the devastating effects it has on its victims. Does God care? Of course, he does. The Psalmist writes, *"The Lord is close to the brokenhearted and saves those who are crushed in spirit" (Psalm 34:18)*. The Psalmist also writes,

"He heals the brokenhearted and binds up their wounds."
(Psalm 147:3)

Friend, you are more valuable than how your abuser treated you when they violated you. You may feel worthless and void of any dignity and respect. You may think that there is no healing from these wounds that run deep into your soul. I wish I had magic words to make it all disappear, but I don't. However, God has given you tears to help you cope. All I can tell you is that your tears are not wasted. Your abuser will not get away with what they did. God will have justice for what was stolen from you. In Christ, you are made new. In Christ, you will receive a new body. In Christ, you have been free to be loosed from the shackles of that shame you didn't ask for. I know you have wept many tears over that injustice, but let God have the last word. Just as all murderers will give an account, so will all sexual perverts. Their only hope is for them to repent and trust in Christ. I know you might struggle with your attacker receiving grace but forgiving them as Christ forgave you is the pathway to true healing. I know that you might want revenge (from a human perspective, and I don't blame you). My counsel to you will be to leave it to God. As Paul told the Romans, *"Do not take revenge, my dear friends, but leave room for God's wrath, for it is written: 'It is mine to avenge; I will repay,' says the Lord." (Romans 12:19)* Your tears will not go unnoticed, for God cares deeply for you.

Although you feel as if your pain will never end,
Let me give you some assurance, my friend,
The Lion of the Tribe of Judah has won the war,
And for this reason, you will one day weep no more.

DISCUSSION QUESTIONS

1. How does the Bible inform our understanding of justice and injustice? What passages or stories from the Bible illustrate God's perspective on these issues?

2. How can individuals who have experienced great suffering, such as murder, racism, or sexual abuse, find healing and hope in God?

3. How can we guard against adopting worldly ideologies and ensure that our pursuit of justice aligns with biblical principles? How does one define justice?

4. How can those who have been abused or oppressed know they are more valuable than their abusers treated them?

5. What future hope is there for those who have been crushed by abusers? What would you say to such person?

CHAPTER 9:
DEATH AND WEEPING

One of my favorite hymns, *It is Well,* was written by Horatio G. Spafford. It has proven to be a timeless classic that continues to reach each generation. The hymn, though, took on new meaning for me when I learned the story behind the words.[36] Spafford was a lawyer and successful businessman in Chicago. He was married to Anna, and they had five children. 1871 was a tragic year for the family as one of their sons died from pneumonia, and they lost much of their business to the great Chicago fire. Two years later the family decided to travel to Europe on an ocean liner. However, a last-minute business problem kept Spafford at home. So, he decided to send his wife and four daughters across the Atlantic planning to meet them just days later.

Four days into the journey, their ship, the Ville du Harve, collided with the Scottish ship, the Loch Earn, in a tragic accident. Anna gathered her four daughters on the top deck, knelt, and prayed, asking God to spare them. However, just twelve minutes later,

---

[36] *What I share here is a summary from the following article that recounts the story. I already knew of the story before reading this article, but I took the facts from this article. https://www.staugustine.com/story/lifestyle/faith/2014/10/17/story-behind-song-it-well-my-soul/985525007/*

the ship sank into the depths of the Atlantic. Entering eternity at that moment were the souls of 226 passengers including the Spafford's four daughters. A sailor rowing a boat near where the ship went down found Anna floating on a piece of the wreckage. He pulled her to safety, and nine days later, she safely reached Wales. Upon her arrival, she sent her husband a wire which began, "Saved alone, what shall I do?" A pastor who also survived this tragedy later recounted hearing Anna testifying, "God gave me four daughters. Now they have been taken away from me. Someday I will understand why."

I can't imagine the pain that Horatio must have felt when he received the news from Anna. The Spaffords, at that point, had lost all five of their children. Upon receiving the news, Spafford booked passage on the next ship to be with his grieving wife. Four days into the journey, the captain of his ship called for Spafford letting him know that they were over the spot where his children had died. What was on his mind at the time? Well, it was after this moment that he began writing his most famous hymn. The first verse tells us how he was handling this tragedy:

"When peace like a river attendeth my way,
When sorrows like sea billows roll.

Whatever my lot, Thou hast taught me to say
It is well, it is well with my soul"[37]

"When sorrows like sea billows roll" – we have all felt the emotion behind that line. I've felt the sting of death many times in my life. As a pastor, I have been at the bedside of many people who have died and have entered eternity. Many of my friends, family, and church members have died. I've had my shoulder cried on and my shirt wet with tears by others. I once slept in the hospital for several days, awaiting the birth of a baby boy who we knew wasn't going to make it. I was there to comfort his parents when he passed. I've had to break the news of death to many people that their loved ones were no longer living. It is one of the most challenging things about being in the ministry. I've seen the heartache and devastation on the faces of many people. I've performed many funerals and memorial services. I've buried believers, and I've also buried people who I knew had rejected Christ even to their last moments on this earth. I hate the feeling that death leaves behind for those who live. Death is real to me.

I'll never forget the pain that sucker-punched Lori and me. Lori was pregnant with our second child. We had just learned this fantastic news and bought a

---

[37] *https://hymnary.org/result/56347343/312808/text/when_peace_like_a_river_allendeth_my_way*

fetal heart monitor. We listened with joy to our baby's heartbeat. We then left for vacation to Williamsburg, Virginia as it was still early in her pregnancy. Just a few days into our vacation, everything abruptly changed. Lori noticed that she was experiencing some unusual symptoms. With much concern, we took her to the hospital only to discover that they were unable to detect a heartbeat in our baby. Lori had had a miscarriage. We were devastated. I remember going back to our room and weeping the rest of the night and all the next day. We packed up our belongings and made the long drive back home. The only thing we wanted at that moment was to hug our only child, Tyler. We picked him up from my parent's house and hugged him tight. Like so many people who have experienced a miscarriage, we never got to hug or kiss our baby. The verse I kept reading again and again was what David said when his child died, *"Can I bring him back again? I shall go to him, but he will not return to me." (2 Samuel 12:23)* Since then, the Lord has blessed us with two additional children. He is good. Perhaps this is the thing that parents fear the most — losing their children. It is perhaps one of my greatest fears.

Many have had to bury their children as death has left its awful sting. It is never easy, and it hurts every time. Lori was still too early in her pregnancy for us to know the gender of our baby. I think about this occasionally, creating a longing for me to see our child.

The only positive aspect of this tragedy is knowing that this child never had to suffer the evils of this world. This child will never know how difficult it is to fight the battle against sin (although they inherited my sinful nature). They only know the glories of heaven and the Lord Jesus. That thought is precious to us and has helped us heal from the pain of the miscarriage. Perhaps you have felt this same pain as well. I know of many couples who have suffered through a miscarriage or the early death of a child. God knows our pain and sees our tears.

Many people fear death. Believers don't worry about dying as far as the state of their souls is concerned. However, many people fear how they are going to die. For the believer, death is not to be feared. As Paul says, he would rather depart and be with Christ *"for that is far better." (Philippians 1:23)* However, from a human standpoint, seeing anything positive about death is difficult. When our loved ones and friends die, it hurts. There is a sort of "sting" that comes into our souls and causes grief, sorrow, and weeping. Yes, death stings. Why does it sting? Paul says, *"The sting of death is sin, and the power of sin is the law." (1 Corinthians 15:56)* Death is the price we must pay because we are sinners born in Adam. *"Therefore, just as sin came into the world through one man, and death through sin, and so death spread to all men because all sinned." (Romans 5:12)* And of course, it is the just payment of our rebellion, *"For the wages of sin is death…" (Romans 6:23)*

Death does not play favorites. Nobody is promised tomorrow. Death doesn't care how young, healthy, old, or safe you are; it takes its victims without prejudice. Everyone has been appointed a time to die. Who gets to determine this time? This is a prerogative of God. This is the only way we can explain why a 100-year-old chain smoker is still alive at this old age. Only God. Also, it is the only explanation as to why the seemingly healthy athlete drops dead of a heart attack. Only God. All we can say in these moments is that it was "their time." Is there such a thing as "their time?" Yes, indeed. In Job, we read, speaking of the life of man, *"Since his days are determined, and the number of his months is with you, and you have appointed his limits that he cannot pass." (Job 14:5)* If you think about it in this way, there is no such thing as an early death. Yes, of course, from a human perspective, indeed, there is. However, if we truly understand that our days are numbered, we know God will take us at the time he has appointed. This means I won't go a second sooner than I'm supposed to, and I won't go a second later. There is a reason why some survive suicide attempts or escape from burning buildings, and the answer is God. Yes, God sometimes even decrees our death through our stupidity. Everybody lives and dies by God's decree; it is humbling. That truth of "their time" might be true, but it's not the balm of the soul that gives relief that someone you loved has died. I've been there, and I hate that feeling every time. The sting of physical death has been felt since Cain murdered Abel. We don't see Adam's and Eve's reaction to his death, but I'm sure it involved weeping. It was something God had warned them about if they disobeyed, and it happened. They lost their son, and I imagine they thought back to God's warning in the garden.

In the Scriptures, we are told of many people who have died. We see the sting of death affect even the greatest of believers. For example, Abraham suffered the sting of death when Sarah died. *"And Sarah died … and Abraham went in to mourn for Sarah and to weep for her." (Genesis 23:2)* Israel felt the sting when their leader Moses died, *"And the people of Israel wept for Moses in the plains of Moab thirty days. Then the days of weeping and mourning for Moses were ended." (Deuteronomy 34:8)* The people wept for death of Jairus daughter, *"They came to the house of the ruler of the synagogue, and Jesus saw a commotion, people weeping and wailing loudly." (Mark 5:38)* Weeping or sorrow is a natural and universal symptom of death.

Do you feel bad that you can't stop crying over one's death? Don't be ashamed, for not even Jesus was immune to weeping and sorrow. One day, Jesus learned that his friend Lazarus was sick. Jesus could have healed him even though he was not in the same town as he. Four days later, Jesus arrived in Bethany, where Lazarus lived, and learned that Lazarus had died. The scene was filled with sorrow. *"Now when Mary came to where Jesus was and saw him, she fell at his feet, saying to him, 'Lord, if you had been here, my brother would not have died.' When Jesus saw her weeping, and the Jews who had come with her also weeping, he was deeply moved in his spirit and greatly troubled. And he said, 'Where have you laid him?' They said to him, 'Lord, come and see.' Jesus wept." (John 11:32–35)* Jesus knew he would raise Lazarus from the dead in just a few moments. However, we are told that he also wept when he saw their sorrow. What does that tell you about your weeping? What does that tell you about your compassion for others?

An old saying goes like this: "The only certainties in life are death and taxes." Friends, if this were true for all of us, we would have every reason to weep and keep on weeping forever. However, for the one who is in Christ, that is not true at all. We can reword that old saying: "The only certainties in life are death and resurrection." This is the truth that Jesus gave to Lazarus' sisters and those in Bethany. *"Jesus said to her, 'I am the resurrection and the life. Whoever believes in me, though he die, yet shall he live, and everyone who lives and believes in me shall never die." (John 11:25–26)* This message of hope is what Paul gave to the Thessalonians, *"But we do not want you to be uninformed, brothers, about those who are asleep, that you may not grieve as others do who have no hope." (1 Thessalonians 4:13)* The word asleep is a euphemism for death. Yes, believers don't have to fear death, for death for a believer does not have the last word. The reason we don't have to continue to weep for our dead friends and family in Christ is the hope of resurrection! The death of a believer is never a goodbye, it is merely a goodnight.

This is why the resurrection of Jesus is the cornerstone of our faith. With a dead Jesus, we are still in our sins and lost forever. However, we as believers will also be raised with Christ to eternal life since Christ has risen. This is why the message changes for those who know Christ: "Weep no more." It is what Jesus says to the widow whose son had died. *"And when the Lord saw her, he had compassion on her and said to her, 'Do not weep. Then he came up and touched the bier, and the bearers stood still. And he said, 'Young man, I say to you, arise.' And the dead man sat up and began to speak, and Jesus gave him to his mother." (Luke 7:14–15)* The reason she does not need to weep anymore is the truth of resurrection!

We see this when those disciples went to the tomb on the morning of the resurrection. They all went in weeping as they prepared to see their dead Lord. Mary wept. *"But Mary stood **weeping** outside the tomb, and as she wept she stooped to look into the tomb." (John 20:11)* The angels greeted her by saying, *"Woman, why are you*

weeping? *" She told them, 'They have taken away my Lord, and I do not know where they have laid him." (John 20:13)* Then Jesus speaks to her, and she doesn't recognize him. *"Jesus said to her, "Woman, why are you **weeping**? Whom are you seeking?" (John 20:15).* Then Jesus reveals himself to her, and she rejoices. Why did her weeping stop? — the resurrection!

The promise of resurrection enables me as a pastor to get through every funeral I do. The most difficult funerals are, of course, for those who I know did not know Jesus. However, even at that moment, the gospel drives me forward with great urgency. For I know that many who are attending that funeral also don't know Jesus. So, I preach and proclaim Christ so they might be saved and have the promise of resurrection. The irony is rich as I preach to dying men who don't know they're already dead, who must realize that they can live now if only they will trust Christ alone. The only thing that keeps me going in these moments is the truth of the resurrection of Christ.

Why does the resurrection give us so much promise? It's because the resurrection of Jesus tells us that there is hope for the future. The resurrection of Jesus tells us that one day we will never feel the sting of death again. This is what Paul says to the Corinthians. *"Behold! I tell you a mystery. We shall not all sleep, but we shall all be changed, in a moment, in the twinkling of an eye, at the last trumpet. For the trumpet will sound, and the dead will be raised imperishable, and we shall be changed. For this perishable body must put on the imperishable, and this mortal body must put on immortality. When the perishable puts on the imperishable, and the mortal puts on immortality, then shall come to pass the saying that is written: 'Death is swallowed up in victory.' 'O death, where is your victory? O death, where is your sting?' The sting of death is sin, and the power of sin is the law. But thanks be to God, who gives us the victory through our Lord Jesus Christ." (1 Corinthians 15:51–57)*

Be encouraged! The sting of death is not forever! There is coming a day in which you will never weep again for those who have died in Christ. Why? For this coming day is a day when nobody in Christ dies again. When will this happen? This will come at "the end." Paul says, *"Then comes the end, when he delivers the kingdom to God the Father after destroying every rule and every authority and power. For he must reign until he has put all his enemies under his feet. The last enemy to be destroyed is death." (1 Corinthians 15:24-26)* Death will be destroyed. Death will be the last thing to die. Amen!

Death must be viewed differently by Christians. It brings to them a dual dose of hope that it doesn't for the rest of the world. Thomas Brooks explains, "A man that sees his propriety in God knows that death shall be the funeral of all his sins, sorrows, afflictions, temptations, desertions, oppositions, vexations, oppressions, and persecutions. And he knows that death shall be the resurrection of his hopes, joys, delights, comforts, and contentments and that it shall bring him to a more clear, full, perfect, and constant enjoyment of God."[38]

Friends, I can't wait for that day. However, until that day comes, God has given us tears for weeping, which is God's gift. We weep, but not in the same way as others who have no hope. Let us worship God through our weeping, as we will inevitably feel the sting of death many times over until Jesus returns for us. Some of us may lose family, friends, or some of our church family before that day. If that day is much farther into the future it may be that our family, friends, and church will weep over us. It's ok. It's going to be ok. Trust me, even though you weep now, you won't always do so, so worship God through those tears and look forward with much hope.

May Spafford's hymn ring true in your heart. It is well, It is well with my soul.

---

[38] Ritzema, Elliot, and Elizabeth Vince, eds. 2013. *300 Quotations for Preachers from the Modern Church*. Pastorum Series. Bellingham, WA: Lexham Press.

Although you feel as if your pain will never end,
Let me give you some assurance, my friend,
The Lion of the Tribe of Judah has won the war,
And for this reason, you will one day weep no more.

DISCUSSION QUESTIONS

1. Have you ever struggled with fear or anxiety about death? How has your faith helped you overcome these feelings? Do you fear death? Why?

2. Why does death exist? Why do we die? How does this give more definition to your mortality?

3. What do you believe about the saying it was just "their time." Do you think God is sovereign over when we die? Why or why not? How does this give you comfort?

4. How does knowing that "Jesus wept" help you when you are grieving over the death of a loved one?

5. How does the hope of resurrection overcome our fear of death and the sting that it leaves?

CHAPTER 10:
PRAYER AND WEEPING

Anyone who has tried to develop a faithful prayer life knows it is difficult work. This is why prayer must be developed as a discipline that grows in holiness and confidence in the Christian life. One of the reasons many don't pray (besides laziness) is that we think we need instant gratification. For example, some may need clarification as to why they have prayed about an item and not had what they desire come to fruition. This is because we need to understand better what prayer is supposed to be in our lives. The purpose of prayer is not for us to get things from God. It is given to us as a way to worship God. Prayer is not about bringing your wish list to God as a child writes a letter to Santa Claus. If that is our attitude in prayer, then we expose what we genuinely worship: ourselves!

Some think that God needs us to pray. No, God doesn't need us to pray as if we are some missing link in the chain of his divine will. God does use our prayers, not because he needs us, but because he is honored. God is self-sufficient in all of his actions and his nature. God's independence from creation was a part of Paul's sermon on Mars Hill. Paul said, *"The God who made the world and everything in it, being Lord of heaven and earth, does not live in temples made by man, nor is he served by human hands, <u>as though he needed anything since he himself</u>*

gives to all mankind life and breath and everything." (Acts 17:24-25)

So why, then, do we pray? If God doesn't need us to pray, then what's the point? Some have asked this question and used it as an excuse not to pray. However, that is not a healthy or biblical view of God's sovereignty in prayer. We must pray because we are commanded to pray. Prayer is more for our benefit than anything. We don't pray because we need God to change his will; we pray to align our wills with God's will. If we could change God's mind with our prayers, then he would not be immutable, and therefore, he would not be God. Prayer, then, is for *our* benefit to express to God what's going on (not that he doesn't already know). For this reason, prayer is often associated with weeping, for we can pour our hearts out before the Lord. Prayer is how we can worship God through our tears. The Scripture is filled with prayers that are filled with tears. The Psalms are filled with accounts of the Psalmist crying out to God as he wept. We need these praying tears as they do wonders for our souls to express what can only come from a broken heart to God.

Other kinds of tears are wrought through prayer, which I want to focus on in this chapter. This prayer is known as intercessory prayer. Intercessory prayer is a prayer that is prayed on behalf of another.

Anytime you pray for someone else, it's intercessory prayer. Paul asked his readers to pray for him and his missionary journeys. For example, *"I appeal to you, brothers, by our Lord Jesus Christ and by the love of the Spirit, to strive together with me in your prayers to God on my behalf…" (Romans 15:30)* He also asked the Colossians, *"Continue steadfastly in prayer, being watchful in it with thanksgiving. At the same time, pray also for us, that God may open a door for the word, to declare the mystery of Christ, on account of which I am in prison." (Colossians 4:3)* Peter, in Acts 12, was arrested and put into prison. However, the church prayed on his behalf until he was miraculously freed. *"So Peter was kept in prison, but earnest prayer for him was made to God by the church." (Acts 12:5)* We are commanded to pray for those in authority over us (1 Timothy 2:12); our enemies (Matthew 5:44); the sick (James 5:14); and all kinds of people (1 Timothy 2:1).

Not all kinds of intercessory prayer involves weeping. I'm not suggesting that you must weep as you pray — no not at all. I am saying that weeping during intercessory prayer happens as we are broken for others. Have you ever prayed for a family member or friend you knew was in big trouble? Perhaps the trajectory of their life didn't look as if it would turn out well because of sinful decisions. So, what do we do? We hit our knees and lift these people up to God. However, as we pray for these people, they sometimes continue to let us down. What do we do then? We fall on our knees in desperation as we don't know to whom else to turn except to God. What about someone on death's door whom you desire to be healed? Have you wept over a sick spouse, someone tragically injured in an accident, or for your precious church family? God sees you and hears you. This is why the church must gather to pray. If your church has a prayer meeting, do your best to attend, pray, and weep together in prayer.

When we pray for people in this way, we must understand that our prayers are not just for them but are also for us. This pain is often felt when a parent has a wayward child. Parents can be prone to feelings of frustration, anger, and even a broken heart for their child. No parent is perfect; all have made mistakes while raising their children. Perhaps some of the child's waywardness results from poor parenting. Nevertheless, parents' hearts are broken when they see children make decisions that they know are not in the best interest of their children. What is a parent to do in these moments? The parent must trust the Lord for the child's well-being and good. No parent can undo the past, but we can all strive forward to pave the pathways our children take. We can guide, direct, encourage, and rebuke, but ultimately, our children must make their own choices. We leave them to the mercy and grace of God. We can't save our kids. All we can do is point them to Jesus, give them the truth, pray, and ask God to be merciful. Many parents have wept for their children. This may involve wisdom, salvation, health, or holiness. May we never stop loving, guiding, protecting, and preaching to them the truth. May your tears be used by God to help you trust him for your children. Never give up on them!

Jeremiah was known as the "weeping prophet." This is because he wept so much throughout his book, and he is filled with sorrow over the sins of his people. He knew how it was to have people close to him sin and be broken in prayer for them. Jeremiah lived during a time when he was preaching against the sins of Judah. He warned them by a word from the Lord that destruction was coming and that they had to repent. He knew that his country was about to be slaughtered, and he was so devastated to see nobody responding and appealing to the grace and mercy of God. So, what did Jeremiah do? Jeremiah prayed for Judah with great tears before God. He said, *"Oh that my head were waters, and my eyes a fountain of tears, that I might weep day and night for the slain of the daughter of my people!" (Jeremiah 9:1)* Jeremiah says again to them, *"But if you will not listen, my soul will weep in secret for your pride; my eyes will weep bitterly and run down with tears because the Lord's flock has been taken captive." (Jeremiah 13:17)* God even told Jeremiah to say, *"You shall say to them this word: 'Let my eyes run down with tears night and day, and let them not cease, for the virgin daughter of my people is shattered with a great wound, with a very grievous blow." (Jeremiah 14:17)*

Who is your "Judah" that you seek God for in your prayers? For whom have you shared many tears? God's command to Jeremiah was that his message would be to them that even though God shatters them, he will not give up. "Oh Judah, I will pray and weep for you night and day." Judah didn't listen to Jeremiah, resulting in his brokenness for them. He had told them the truth, but their hearts were so hardened by sin that it fell upon deaf ears. When did you last tell your Judah that you were praying for them? They may not receive your weeping and prayers well, but it may lead to their repentance. Show them you sincerely care for them and are broken over their rejection of God.

God did judge Judah by sending Nebuchadnezzar to destroy Jerusalem, to kill and enslave many of them. Those who were enslaved were taken away from their land to Babylon. It was there they spent almost seventy years away from their home. New generations were born in Babylon who had never seen Jerusalem. One of those taken as a captive was a young man named Daniel. Daniel was a blessing to the captives in Babylon as God used him to encourage them. Like Joseph, Daniel was made to be high in command underneath their captors. God had told them through the prophets that they would be away for seventy years. So, as the seventy years were ending, Daniel began to wonder how God would rescue his people. So, what did Daniel do? Daniel offered an intercessory prayer on behalf of the captives. Daniel was in great sorrow as he saw the end of the Babylonian reign now turn into a Persian one. So, how long will his people be away from the land? What does Daniel do? *"Then I turned my face to the Lord God, seeking him by prayer and pleas for mercy with fasting and sackcloth and ashes." (Daniel 9:3)*

Daniel sought God in prayer with "sackcloth and ashes," which was a symbol of mourning. Daniel prayed, and I'm sure he wept as he considered the weightiness of their captivity. Daniel not only confessed his sin but also the sins of his people. God answered Daniel's prayer by giving him the vision of the seventy weeks. God's answer was not necessarily what Daniel asked God for, but it was the answer he needed to hear. God ensured that in this seventy-week prophecy, they would return home, but it would not be easy. These seventy weeks would result in the arrival of the Messiah and the Messianic age. Their temple would be rebuilt, but it would be desecrated again and made desolate. God answers prayer not in the way we always want him to but in the way we always need him to. Our tears should not solely be for our deliverance from our troubles but also for our development.

Years later, the weeping continued through a man named Nehemiah. Nehemiah was the cupbearer to the king of Persia. He was a Jew whom God used to secure his people back in the land by rebuilding the walls. Upon hearing a report on the status of Jerusalem, while living far away, Nehemiah writes, *"As soon as I heard these words I sat down and wept and mourned for days, and I continued fasting and praying before the God of heaven. And I said, "O LORD God of heaven, the great and awesome God who keeps covenant and steadfast love with those who love him and keep his commandments, let your ear be attentive and your eyes open to hear the prayer of your servant that I now pray before you day and night for the people of Israel your servants, confessing the sins of the people of Israel, which we have sinned against you. Even I and my father's house have sinned." (Nehemiah 1:4–6)*

Nehemiah was crushed over the condition of his home and the fact that the walls had not been reconstructed. This meant that those who escaped the wrath of Nebuchadnezzar were still living in the area and were in great danger. So, what did Nehemiah do? He prayed on behalf of these people with weeping and sorrow. Per God's will, it was time to send his people back as promised so that they could be established back in Jerusalem. God answered Nehemiah's prayer in the way Nehemiah desired. However, that's not the way it always works.

You can spend years in prayer seeking God, heartbroken over someone or something, and have it all destroyed anyway. I don't pretend to know why he sometimes does it that way. However, I can confidently say this: God never fails to answer our prayers "our way" when they are in accordance with his will. Sometimes, that person we prayed for doesn't get healed. Sometimes, that person that we have wept for doesn't come to faith in Jesus. Sometimes, the wayward child doesn't return home in repentance. In these "non-answers", we trust God all the more, as our weeping will soon turn into rejoicing when we see all that God has done and how it was good.

Nevertheless, in our weeping-saturated prayers, God can teach, sanctify, and mold us into the people we ought to be. Those tears produce healing as we rest in God's providence and know that he is indeed good. Intercessory prayer is of the utmost importance not just for the person or people we pray for but also for us who do the praying. How important is this in the life of a believer? Well, not doing it would mean being disobedient to God. How often have we told someone, "I'll pray for you," but then don't? Sometimes, we throw that term around as if it's nothing but a good luck charm. May it never be so, friends!

Another intercessory prayer that causes weeping is praying for the salvation of those close to us. We all have family and friends who don't know Christ. If you have never shared Christ with them, then do so. It is heartbreaking when we encounter someone who doesn't know the Lord. However, it hits closest to home when it is someone in our tight circle. Paul knew this pain, and he felt it for the Jewish people. Paul wrote to the Romans, "*I am speaking the truth in Christ—I am not lying; my conscience bears me witness in the Holy Spirit—that I have great sorrow and unceasing anguish in my heart. For I could wish that I were accursed and cut off from Christ for the sake of my brothers, my kinsmen according to the flesh.*" (Romans 9:1–3) Paul prayed for the Jewish people to believe, making it his mission. When Paul entered a new town or city, he first went to the Jews and shared the gospel with them. Paul was heartbroken over so many of his Jewish brothers who were blinded from seeing the glories of God in the face of Jesus Christ. However, he didn't just pray for their salvation, he also shared Christ with them. May we do the same!

May our weeping for others be found to be driven in prayer, whether it be for their physical ailments, salvation, waywardness, repentance, or even the condition of our nation. May we never be afraid to kneel and intercede for others. This is what God has called us to do. God may answer your prayer as you desire because he is faithful, and your prayer might be a part of his will to accomplish what he desires. This is the example of the Lord Jesus. In John 17, Jesus offered up his "high priestly prayer" as he prayed for his disciples. This same night, Jesus labored in prayer with great agony, sweating as if it were great drops of blood (see Luke 22:44). It was before this prayer that he tells his disciples, *"My soul is very sorrowful, even to death; remain here, and watch with me." (Matthew 26:38)* Jesus practiced intercessory prayer while on this earth. He even prayed for those who had crucified and flogged him. While hanging on the cross, Jesus prayed, *"Father, forgive them, for they do not know what they are doing." (Luke 23:34)* Not only did Jesus pray for others while he was on earth, but he also continued to do so in heaven. *"Consequently, he is able to save to the uttermost those who draw near to God through him, since he always lives to make intercession for them." (Hebrews 7:25)* Not only Christ in heaven but the Holy Spirit prays for us on our behalf here as we pray (see Romans 8:26). Our Lord took on the arduous task of sorrowful prayers, and so should we. Interceding for others is difficult, even for those that involve tears. Don't give up. Pray for others and give them over to the Lord. Use your tears as worship as you depend on God for whatever he decides to do and know that he can't be wrong. We will keep praying these prayers until we die or the world ends.

Although you feel as if your pain will never end,
Let me give you some assurance, my friend,
The Lion of the Tribe of Judah has won the war,
And for this reason, you will one day weep no more.

DISCUSSION QUESTIONS

1. In what ways can we guard against viewing prayer as a means to "get things from God," and instead approach it as a way to align our will with His?

2. How do tears play a role in our prayers, particularly in intercessory prayer? How can we learn to embrace our emotions, including sorrow and brokenness, in our prayer life?

3. The chapter mentions that one of the reasons people do not pray is because they expect instant gratification. Do you think this is true in your own prayer life or in the lives of those around you?

4. The chapter mentions that prayer is more for our benefit than for God's, as it aligns our will with His. How does prayer shape your understanding of God's will for your life?

5. The chapter emphasizes the importance of praying for others, even when it is difficult or involves tears. How can we cultivate a heart of compassion and intercession for those around us?

CHAPTER 11:
BETRAYAL AND WEEPING

Opening yourself up to those you love and care about is a rewarding and needful aspect of our lives. Giving these pieces of our hearts to others draws us closer, and these bonds are beautiful and bring glory to God. We need to have these kinds of relationships in our lives. It is with these people we share our deepest secrets and allow them to enter parts of our lives that we have not let others into. These relationships surpass superficial conversations such as "How's the weather?" or jokes and funny stories. These relationships are special bonds of love and trust, which are more intimate. Although these close relationships are needed, it is devastating when this trust is violated and the pieces of our hearts are shattered. Betrayal from the hands of our family, ministry partners, friends, spouses, children, and church family is bound to happen in this broken world. The Scriptures are not silent when it comes to this issue. Several in the Bible went through betrayal at the hands of those close to them. We can find solace in their pain and comfort that we are not alone.

The Apostle Paul had many who served with him as partners in ministry. Of course, some of the most well-known were Timothy, Silas, Barnabas, and Luke. He was close to these men, and they served together well over time. However, Paul tells us that one of these men, Demas, abandoned him. We don't know much about Demas except that he was with Paul. He is mentioned twice as one who sent greetings to the church (Colossians 4:14) and (Philemon 1:24). Demas went from being Paul's trusted ministry partner to being one who betrayed him. Paul wrote to Timothy, *"For Demas, in love with this present world, has deserted me and gone to Thessalonica." (2 Timothy 4:10)* We are not told any specifics, but that Demas was "in love" with this present world. Paul wrote this letter to Timothy while he was in prison in Rome. This epistle is one of the last things Paul wrote before being beheaded for the gospel. He was ready to die, and at his most desperate hour, he faced a betrayal of the highest magnitude. Although possible, we are not told that Paul wept over Demas. However, we know Demas' departure had Paul longing for Timothy to come to his side. Paul told Timothy, *"Do your best to come to me soon." (2 Timothy 4:9)* Only Luke remained with Paul in Rome during his imprisonment. The rest of Paul's companions, who were close by, didn't stand with him. He wrote to Timothy, *"At my first defense no one came to stand by me, but all deserted me. May it not be charged against them!" (2 Timothy 4:16)*

It is difficult to understand unless you've been in ministry, but many pastors suffer from loneliness. How can this be? The pastor always has people around him calling and listening to him, right? Loneliness doesn't happen because there is a shortage of people but because there is a lack of meaningful relationships. How and why does this happen? It occurs first from caution and the nature of the calling. I've grown close to other pastors in my town throughout my ministry. However, some of those pastors and I have drifted apart theologically or have another kind of disagreement that makes a meaningful partnership in the gospel difficult. I don't know the exact pain that Paul endured at the hands of Demas. However, I do know of similar pain. This happens when members of my church leave. That is just a reality of pastoral ministry. Only some people who come will stay with you. Not everyone who comes will feel the same way about you that you do about them. This is especially true when those you are supposed to be close to leave for no valid reason. I'm not talking about when people move away, but when people hurt you, betray you, and or lie about you. This has happened to me. This pain has led me to build walls that make future friendships difficult because of the fear of being hurt again in a similar way. Whenever trust has been violated, giving that same level of confidence to someone else is always challenging. Over the last twenty-five years, this has happened more times than I want to admit, and it is devastating every time.

Sometimes, the only connections that some pastors have with their congregations are when their church members need them. Some even get upset with their pastor when he is "not there" for them, never considering how they were never there for their pastor. Many pastors don't make it long-term in the ministry; burnout is real. This is because often the pastor is always the one who gives and not always the one who receives. This is why a plurality of elders is crucial, not only for the church but also for the pastors at the church. So, with all that being said, please care for your pastors well, especially if your church lacks a plurality of elders. Your pastor also needs friendships, care, love, and prayers from his congregation. He needs you more than you think he does. He needs to laugh and receive from you as much as he gives you. Pastors are called to be shepherds, but they are also sheep. How do you ensure your pastor is appropriately cared for? Your pastor doesn't always need you to be a church member to him. He needs you to be a faithful friend.

At the end of his ministry, Paul felt desertion from others. How did Paul manage to maintain his sanity? Paul needed friends, so he called for Timothy and Mark to come to his side. Paul had another friend who stuck close to him, "*But the Lord stood by me and strengthened me so that through me the message might be fully proclaimed and all the Gentiles might hear it. So, I was rescued from the lion's mouth. The Lord will rescue me from every evil deed and bring me safely into his heavenly kingdom. To him be the glory forever and ever. Amen" (2 Timothy 4:17-18)* If you are a pastor, you know what I speak of, be encouraged, and cast your confidence in Christ alone, although you feel alone. Your tears are not for nothing. He will see you through these times of betrayal, loneliness, and being disconnected from those you've been called to care for. Perhaps you have always been kind to your pastor. We praise God for people like you who care for pastors well.

I'm grateful to be a part of a loving church family. However, even in the most loving church families, sheep bite, and the wounds go deep when they do. Over the last twenty-five years of ministry, it has happened enough for me to act defensively. Sadly, some will support you only to achieve an agenda or to get something from you. Some will love you and become family, only to discard you at the drop of a hat. Sadly, these hurts will come and are par for the course in pastoral ministry. The same people whom a pastor has been called to love don't always love him the way he loves them. The people who want you to be there for them don't always consider that they must be there for you. These blows of ministry have caused many a pastor to quit altogether. Many of my sorrows in ministry have made me ponder walking away more than once. However, that's when I remembered that the ministry was filled with sinners such as myself.

I consider the Lord Jesus, who was betrayed, denied by his closest friends, and rejected by his own, and he still was faithful to serve his Father with joy. If the Lord Jesus didn't experience a "perfect" ministry on earth, what gives me that right? One of my college professors once joked, "The ministry would be perfect if there were no people," but then he said, "but then there would be no ministry." Perhaps this is why John Newton described pastoral ministry as "a sorrow filled with joy."[39] The Apostle Paul had a similar sentiment when he described the hardships of his ministry, which are multiplied a hundred times more than I can ever experience. Paul says that despite these hardships, he is *"sorrowful, yet always rejoicing." (2 Corinthians 6:10)* Yes, my friends, even though I have had great losses of friends, church members, and sleep, Jesus is worth it. I am owed no loyalty, allegiance, or friendship by any individual. I am a wretched man who knows the depths of my sins and failures.

One of the most painful betrayals happens within our own family. The relationship that ought to be the dearest is between a husband and wife. However, the sin that often fractures this union is the sin of adultery. Adultery is a betrayal that breaks hearts and deeply wounds not just the offended spouse but all those connected with them (family, friends, church).

---

[39] *https://ftc.co/resource-library/blog-entries/john-newtons-pastoral-poem/*

Far too many tears have been shed over the sin of adultery. This pain leaves a tsunami of confusion, a lack of self-worth, and sometimes a lifetime of guilt for both parties. Whether you are reading this as the one who committed adultery (and hopefully repented) or the one who was sinned against, let me assure you that your tears are not for nothing. We pray that restoration has happened in your situation, although I understand that is not always possible. However, we praise God when healing and restoration happen through the gospel's power. This is the outcome we desire to have in all of these cases. Even though forgiving is difficult, we should always forgive when repentance has occurred. We don't want to hold the sins of those who have offended us in this way against them if Christ has forgiven them. When repentance happens, we must not keep these charges against our brothers and sisters, as those who must wear scarlet letters for the rest of their lives. If they are in Christ, their sins have been removed from them as far as the East is from the West.

The sin of adultery is seen in the Old Testament as the nation of Israel was repeatedly unfaithful to God. Israel continued to worship other gods and adopt the deities of foreign nations. Israel was regarded as the "wife" of the LORD. In Isaiah 54:5, God says to her, "*For your Maker is your husband, the LORD of hosts is his name; and the Holy One of Israel is your Redeemer, the God of the whole earth he is called.*" Although she was in covenant with God, she acted the part of an unfaithful wife who welcomed other lovers in her bed. God gave a scolding rebuke and a vivid description in Ezekiel 16:15-34. He also says through Jeremiah to Israel, *"Surely, as a treacherous wife leaves her husband, so have you been treacherous to me, O house of Israel, declares the Lord." (Jeremiah 3:20)*

For those whom the sin of adultery has wounded, you might ask, is there anyone who can understand my pain? Yes, the Lord does. God told Ezekiel that he was broken over their betrayal. *"I have been broken over their whoring heart that has departed from me and over their eyes that go whoring after their idols." (Ezekiel 6:9)* God knows the pain of adultery but also knows that he must be faithful to his promise. Strangely, he teaches the nation this lesson by asking Hosea to marry a promiscuous woman (Gomer). Hosea does, and Gomer had children with other men while still married to Hosea. All of this was to show the nation through Hosea how their sin had affected their relationship with God. God said through Hosea, *"My heart recoils within me; my compassion grows warm and tender." (Hosea 11:8)* Yes, God knows the pain of unfaithfulness, and his heart is bent toward restoration. Your tears are not wasted, nor is your pain unsympathized.

Betrayal by a spouse is devastating, but so also is betrayal at the hands of a close friend or child. David had this pain in his life as his son Absalom conspired against him. Absalom usurped his father's throne and overthrew him as king. David had fled for his life under the reign of King Saul and now was fleeing again at the hands of his son. Absalom was able to gain the support of many and plotted against his father. When David heard about Absalom's actions, he fled the city for his life. He climbed the nearby Mount of Olives. We are told, *"But David went up the ascent of the Mount of Olives, weeping as he went, barefoot and with his head covered. And all the people who were with him covered their heads, and they went up, weeping as they went." (2 Samuel 15:30)* Not only had his son turned against him, but so had Ahithophel, one of David's chief advisors. The story turned even more tragic as Joab, one of David's commanders, killed Joab, going against David's wishes. The account says, *"And the king was deeply moved and went up to the chamber over the gate and wept. And as he went, he said, 'O my son Absalom, my son, my son Absalom! Would I had died instead of you, O Absalom, my son, my son!" (2 Samuel 18:33)*

These accounts are too eerily familiar considering what happened hundreds of years later: a Son of David would be at the foot of the Mount of Olives praying in great agony as he was to be betrayed. Jesus had just finished the last supper with his disciples and told Judas to do what needed to be done. Satan had filled Judas to betray Jesus for thirty pieces of silver. Judas showed the chief leaders where Jesus was so that he could be arrested under the cover of the night. Judas had been with Jesus for his entire three-year ministry. Judas was the treasurer of the group, responsible for keeping the money bag. He was one of those whom Jesus called and said, "Follow me." Of course, Jesus knew this was to happen as it was prophesied (Psalm 41:9; Zechariah 11:12-13). Nonetheless, it was still painful. Jesus then went to the garden and prayed and wept over all the looming events about to unfold.

To whom, then, are we able to turn for help? Who can understand our pain? Listen to the words of J.C. Ryle. "The Lord Jesus is just the Savior that the suffering and sorrowful need. He knows well what we mean when we tell Him in prayer of our troubles. He can sympathize with us, when we cry to Him under cruel persecution. Let us keep nothing back from Him. Let us make Him our bosom friend. Let us pour out our hearts before Him. He has had great experience of affliction."[40]

Have you ever been betrayed? God knows, and he cares. The betrayal may have left you untrusting of others, a little more skeptical, and less likely to open your heart as you once did before. Do not lose heart,

---

[40] *Ritzema, Elliot, and Elizabeth Vince, eds. 2013. 300 Quotations for Preachers from the Modern Church. Pastorum Series. Bellingham, WA: Lexham Press.*

for there is hope for those who have been betrayed. We must realize that as long as we live in a broken world, we will be hurt again by others. Again, we must look to the Lord, who knows and understands our pain. We look to the day that all betrayal, adultery, and loneliness will be over. That day is coming soon, my friends. Your tears of betrayal are not for nothing and will soon be wiped away by our God's gracious and kind hand. Rest in him!

> Although you feel as if your pain will never end,
> Let me give you some assurance, my friend,
> The Lion of the Tribe of Judah has won the war,
> And for this reason, you will one day weep no more.

DISCUSSION QUESTIONS

1. How do you think betrayal affects our ability to trust others in the future? Is it possible to fully trust again after experiencing betrayal?

2. What do you think Paul means by his statement in 2 Corinthians 6:10 that we are "sorrowful yet always rejoicing"?

3. Reflecting on David's experience with Absalom, how can we navigate the complexities of family relationships when faced with betrayal or conflict?

4. How can we discern when it is appropriate to rebuild trust in a relationship after betrayal, and when it is necessary to set boundaries or walk away?

5. It is both needful and rewarding to open ourselves up to others. How do we protect our hearts from being shattered by betrayal?

CHAPTER 12:
REPENTANCE AND WEEPING

He was not supposed to stay home but instead was to go to battle with his troops. This was because it was spring, and it was the custom for the kings to go out to battle. However, David did not go, but instead stayed home in Jerusalem. His troops went and *"ravaged the Ammonites and besieged Rabbah." (2 Samuel 11:1)* So, what's the big deal? He's the king. Does he not have the authority to stay home if he desires? Probably, but staying home when he wasn't supposed to put David in a very precarious situation. The first two words of the following verse are loaded. *"It happened late one afternoon..."*. It happened. *It* doesn't take much for *it* to happen. "*It*" can be whatever in your life is caused by your indiscretion and weakness. How did *it* happen?

Well, one afternoon after waking up from a nap, *"walking on the roof of the king's house, that he saw from the roof a woman bathing; and the woman was very beautiful." (2 Samuel 11:2)* The *"it"* in David's life was his lusting after a married woman after having seen her taking a bath. Yes, *"it"* just happens that quickly, and you must be on guard. For men, most cases of adultery begin with their eyes as a woman's appearance attracts them. Women are also prone to *"it"* by a myriad of temptations as well. It doesn't take long to find ourselves caving to our *"it."* It's not a matter of whether we will sin but what we will do when we do sin. What did David do when he saw her? He acted on his lust, brought her to his room, and committed adultery. *"So David sent messengers and took her, and she came to him, and he lay with her." (2 Samuel 11:4)*

There is something about sin that makes us want to hide. This is natural, as sin reminds us of the shame and devastation it leaves behind. Not only do we hide but we also attempt to cover up our sins by lying or erasing the record of our wrongdoings. This is as old as time itself. This is why the man watching pornography deletes his internet history. This is why a couple committing adultery sneaks away to a hotel far outside the city limits. This is why a murderer buries his victims, or the thief creates an alibi to explain why he is not the crook. This is why we tell lies to cover up other lies. It's the same reason why cockroaches scatter when the light comes on. Sin is filled with darkness; it hates light the most.

Sin makes us want to cover up for fear of being exposed. If you name the sin, there will be a propensity to hide it. The fearful thing about our society is the need for many people not to sin in secret. For many, there is no need to cover up their sins as they flaunt them before others with pride. What was evil for centuries is now being accepted and tolerated as good. For these people, God has a strong message, *"Woe to those who call evil good and good evil, who put darkness for light and light for darkness, who put bitter for sweet and sweet for bitter!" (Isaiah 5:20)*

This is the first thing Adam and Eve did after sinning against God. *"Then the eyes of both were opened, and they knew that they were naked. And they sewed fig leaves together and made themselves loincloths." (Genesis 3:7)* Up until this point, Adam and Eve were naked but didn't know it. Why? This is because there was no shame in them. After all, there was no sin in them. However, they first realized a sense of nakedness after sin. Nakedness is a picture of being exposed to who we indeed are. This is something that terrifies most of us. If people knew the real us, what would they think of us? So, in order to hide who we are, we try to cover up our shame, insecurities, and inadequacies by any means possible to keep others from knowing the truth. This is why we awake in the middle of the night after having the "naked" dream. Have you ever had one of those? Or perhaps you dreamed of being in a public place but suddenly realized you were not fully clothed or were in your underwear. We awake in terror, don't we? Why? Because it's the fear of being exposed.

We do all we can to keep others from knowing the real us, and sometimes we think we are so clever as to keep God from knowing. Doesn't that sound foolish? God already knows we are "naked" despite our best efforts to cover up our sins. How did Adam and Eve cover up their nakedness? They sewed fig leaves together. Adam and Eve were not trying to make a fashion statement (remember, there was nobody besides them); they were trying to hide their sin from God. Somehow, we believe we can hide our sins from God as we do with others. How foolish this is, Adam and Eve soon found they couldn't trick God. *"And they heard the sound of the LORD God walking in the garden in the cool of the day, and the man and his wife hid themselves from the presence of the LORD God among the trees of the garden." (Genesis 3:8)*

When Bathsheba left David's house, she left as a pregnant woman. She didn't know it until later, but when she knew, she told David. What did David do? Did he repent of his sin? Did he seek forgiveness from God? No, David did what Adam and Eve did. He sewed his version of "fig leaves" to cover up his "nakedness" by inviting her husband home from battle to sleep with her so nobody would know the truth (See 2 Samuel 11:6-13). When her husband did not oblige, David ordered him to the front of the battle where death would be inevitable (2 Samuel 11:14-17). In case one doesn't know, fig leaves are not a foolproof way of hiding your unmentionables. The fig leaves will soon dry out and wither; soon you'll find yourself replacing one set of decaying fig leaves for another. When we cover up our sins, instead of letting ourselves be exposed before God, we commit a great injustice to our souls. We deceive ourselves with our best attempts by covering up our sins.

God could see right through David's fig leaves, so, the Lord sent Nathan, the prophet, to tell David a story that would confront David in his sin (see 2 Samuel 12:1-6). David was enraged at the story, not realizing the story was about what he had done, until Nathan the prophet exclaims, *"You are the man." (2 Samuel 11:7)* The look on David's face was likely one of horror and grief. David knew he had been caught despite his best efforts at "sewing fig leaves." What was David to do now? He knew there was nowhere else to hide, and the Lord had seen his nakedness. David surrenders and says, *"I have sinned against the Lord." (2 Samuel 12:13)* David uses manipulation to try and cover up his sin, but when he realizes his sin, he confesses and repents. David deserved to die that day. Not only was he guilty of adultery, but also of murder and deceitfulness. Did David die that day? No, he did not. Nathan told him, *"The LORD also has put away your sin; you shall not die. Nevertheless, because by this deed you have utterly scorned the LORD, the child who is born to you shall die." (2 Samuel 12:13–14)* Why did the child have to die? That seems unfair from a human perspective. That is not a question I can answer, but I know that God is good, nonetheless. It's also a reminder that there is always a consequence to our sins. Our sin never just affects us; it also affects others around us. The child dying is a reminder of the wages of sin that began in the garden. No amount of "fig leaves" can cover up our sins.

It's interesting to note that there was also a required death in the garden. Adam and Eve deserved to die for their sin, but God had sacrificed an animal and clothed them in its skins. *"And the LORD God made for Adam and for his wife garments of skins and clothed them." (Genesis 3:21)* This is, of course a picture of what God would do for us in the gospel by sending Jesus. Although we deserve to die for our sins, Christ died for us in our place. He then clothes us in the righteousness of Christ, which covers our shame and sin. What are we to make of these things? Sin destroys, kills, and ruins people. The question is not whether we will sin but what we will do with our sins. We must repent of our sins and run to our Savior. Any professing believer who has no regard for his sin is a person who proves he is no believer at all. In these cases, church discipline is necessary for the love of that person and his soul (See 1 Corinthians 5).

What does repentance look like? David's sincerity made him a man after God's own heart. David knew that his sin was grave. He confessed it to God with great brokenness and weeping. We see David's heartfelt repentance beautifully written in Psalm 51. As

David sings this psalm, I can see tears flowing down his cheek as he cries out to the Lord. He pleads for God's mercy in verse 1, asking God to *"blot out my transgressions."* He asks God to wash and cleanse him from his sin in verse 2. He knows how sin is haunting him day and night, and it won't go away unless he deals with it in verse 3. He takes responsibility for his sin in verse 4 and doesn't blame Bathsheba or anyone else. He takes full responsibility for his actions. He shows how much sin has broken him in verse 7, saying that he is vile and dirty. He desires once again to be "whiter than snow." He also knows that sin has robbed him of joy and gladness and asks God to restore what sin has stolen from him. He asks God for a new heart and a right spirit in verse 10. With a new heart and spirit, David knows he is less likely to commit the same sin again. He then wants his life to be an example so that other people will see the way to God. Ultimately, David knows he cannot worship his way out of sin through feelings or by singing songs that make him feel good. David knows that no amount of good work can make up for what he has done. He understands that what God desires is *"a broken spirit; a broken and contrite heart, O God, you will not despise." (Psalm 51:17)*

When it comes to repentance, weeping is a proper response. Yes, some could offer God "fake tears." Yes, many are just sorry that they got caught and not that they had committed the sin. Yes, many also aren't genuinely repentant and will run back to the same vomit repeatedly. For those who are not remorseful and are not broken over sin as God is, I do not say "weep no more," I say "weep some more!" Weep some more was God's message to Judah in Isaiah 22. The people of Judah had defied God, sinned egregiously, and were on the verge of receiving God's swift judgment. God had told them that it had become inevitable for them to weep. Many in the nation would die, and the rest would be taken as slaves. The temple of God would be destroyed, as well as the city walls, homes, and markets. Years had passed with Judah's being content in their sin, but God says, *"In that day the Lord God of hosts called for weeping and mourning, for baldness and wearing sackcloth."* (Isaiah 22:12) The message was "Oh, Judah, in that day you had better weep." They certainly did, but it was too late to receive God's mercy. This weeping over this judgment is seen through the eyes of the "weeping prophet" Jeremiah. Jeremiah writes in Lamentations 2:11, *"My eyes are spent with weeping; my stomach churns; my bile is poured out to the ground because of the destruction of the daughter of my people, because infants and babies faint in the streets of the city."* The prophet Joel also called for Judah to repent. Joel prophesies, *"Yet even now,"* declares the Lord, *"return to me with all your heart, with fasting, with weeping, and with mourning." (Joel 2:12)* Perhaps you haven't properly wept or sorrowed over your sins because you've never been converted? Yes, you may have "walked an aisle" or repeated the so-called "sinner's prayer." I'm not asking you if you have mentally acknowledged the facts about Christ; I'm asking if you have trusted Christ over the severity of your sin and his sacrifice. Becoming born again involves sorrow for your sin. If you have made a "decision" for Jesus but your life has never changed, how can you say you truly know him?

Once again, I refer to the classic *Pilgrim's Progress*, which is always helpful. We first meet Christian with this description. "a man clothed with rags standing in a certain place, with his face from his own house, a Book in his hand, and a great burden upon his back. I looked, and saw him open the Book and read therein; and as he read he wept and trembled; and not being able longer to contain, he break out with a lamentable cry, saying: 'What shall I do?"[41] Christian began to grow a burden on his back by reading the "Book." The book is, of course, God's word, and his burden is a picture of his sin. Christian lives in the city of Destruction and knows that because of this burden, he will be destroyed in the coming judgment. He desires to rid himself of the burden but doesn't know how to do so. So, what does he do? He wept when he realized his sinful condition.

---

[41] Bunyan, John, *Pilgrim's Progress*, Moody Bible Institute (Chicago, Il) 2007 edition, pg 13

Christian then meets many characters who encourage and discourage him on his journey. However, it was Evangelist who pointed him through the narrow gate on his way to discovering a relief from his burden. This burden was not just a small problem for Christian, it was indeed heinous to him. When warned of all the difficulties that lay on the road ahead by "Mr. Wordly Wiseman," he said, "Why, sir, this burden upon my back is more terrible to me than all these things which you have mentioned, nay, methinks I care not what I meet with in the way, if so be I can also meet with deliverance from my burden."

Yes, Christian was more concerned about his burden than living a comfortable life. This, of course, points the reader to examine their faith in Christ. No true Christian desires to cling to their sin. True repentance is evidenced in us when we hate our sins more than anything else and then take action to leave it behind. Christian didn't care what he had to endure on the journey ahead, nothing could be worse than this burden. Christian's journey through the narrow gate eventually took him to a cross on top of a hill with an open tomb at the bottom. As Christian approached the cross, his burden fell off his back and rolled down the hill into the empty tomb. How does Christian respond? "Now, as he stood looking and weeping… Christian gave three leaps for joy, and went on singing:

> Thus far did I come laden with my sin;
> Nor could aught ease the grief that I was in,
> Till I came hither: what a place is this!
> Must here be the beginning of my bliss?
> Must here the burden fall from off my back?
> Must here, the strings that bound it to me crack?
> Blest cross! blest sepulcher!
> Blest rather be The Man
> that there was put to shame for me!"[42]

God doesn't want you to stop weeping until you have wept over your sin. We will explore why we can stop weeping for our sins in the next chapter, but for now, we ask God to give us more repenting tears. Woe to all the preachers who fail to preach repentance to their people. They lead them on flowery beds of ease that leads to hell. Oh, sinner, weep some more! Weep and keep weeping until you leave sin behind. One of my favorite Puritan authors, Thomas Watson, wrote about his country: "England is an island encompassed by two oceans, an ocean of water, and an ocean of wickedness. O that it may be encompassed with a third ocean, that of repenting tears."[43] Yes, Lord, and may it be true in my country, the United States of America.

---

[42] *Bunyan, John, Pilgrim's Progress, Moody Bible Institute (Chicago, Il) 2007 edition, pg 52-53*

[43] *Watson, Thomas, The Doctrine of Repentance, The Banner of Truth Trust, (Carlisle, PA) 2016, 65*

Watson also wrote, "There is no rowing to paradise except upon the stream of repenting tears."[44] Tears do not equal true repentance, but it's impossible to have true repentance without true brokenness and, yes, even some weeping. This is what many of the Puritans referred to this as a godly sorrow. John Owen said this of godly sorrow: "Godly sorrow will constantly incite the mind unto all duties, acts, and fruits of repentance whatever; it is never barren nor heartless, but being both a grace and a duty, it will stir up the soul unto the exercise of all graces and the performance of all duties that are of the same kind. This the apostle declares fully (2 Cor. 7:11). This therefore is another thing which belongs unto that state of repentance which faith will bring the soul unto and whereby it will evidence itself...And indeed, if this sorrow be constant and operative, there is no clearer evidence in us of saving faith. They are blessed who thus mourn."[45]

This godly sorrow should lead to humility as we worship our Holy God. When godly sorrow produces in us genuine repentance, we can sing as Horatio Spafford wrote,

---

[44] *Watson, Thomas, The Doctrine of Repentance, The Banner of Truth Trust, (Carlisle, PA) 2016, Pg 63*

[45] *Smith, Dale W, Ore from the Puritans' Mine, Reformation Heritage Books, Grand Rapids, MI) 2020, pg. 539*

> "My sin O the bliss
> Of this glorious tho't
> My sin not in part but the whole
> Is nailed to the cross
> And I bear it no more
> Praise the Lord
> Praise the Lord O my soul"[46]

Friends, one of the glories of eternal life is the blessing that we will no longer sin. I'm glad that there is a day coming when I will repent for the last time. There is coming a day in which I will not fail to obey God in all of his commands. This day is not coming because I made myself perfect but because he finished the work in me. His sanctifying presence saved me, is saving me, and will save me. One day, my sin will be non-existent! However, until that day, I pray God causes me to weep some more until he finishes his perfect work in me.

> Although you feel as if your pain will never end,
> Let me give you some assurance, my friend,
> The Lion of the Tribe of Judah has won the war,
> And for this reason, you will one day weep no more.

---

[46] *Bliss, Philip P. "It Is Well with My Soul." Hymns of Faith. Chicago: Hope Publishing Company, 1929, Hymn #143*

DISCUSSION QUESTIONS

1. Reflect on a time when you faced temptation and succumbed to sin. What were the consequences, and how did you respond? Did you try to hide or cover up your sin? How did you eventually come to repentance? What do you need to repent of now?

2. Consider the concept of "godly sorrow" and its role in repentance. How does genuine sorrow over sin differ from worldly sorrow? How can we cultivate a deeper sense of sorrow for our sins?

3. What is your "it," and how can you protect yourself from falling for its temptations? What radical measures are necessary to guard your life?

4. Consider the examples of repentance and weeping in the Bible, such as David in Psalm 51 or the prodigal son in Luke 15. How do these stories illustrate the connection between repentance and emotional response?

5. How can we cultivate a heart that is open to repentance and responsive to the conviction of the Holy Spirit, even to the point of tears? What

practices or attitudes can help us maintain a posture of repentance in our lives?

CHAPTER 13:
GUILT AND WEEPING

The hope and blessing with the promise of "weep no more" only comes after we "weep some more." Why is this true? For true hope in this life is found only in the sweetness and joy of Christ's sufficiency. The old saying is that "time heals all wounds." However, that is not true at all. Time does have a way of numbing our pain, just as my toe doesn't hurt the same as it did the moment I stubbed it. However, for true healing to happen, the mourner must *"taste and see that the LORD is good." (Psalm 34:18)* We must come to realize that Christ is the answer to every pain in our hearts. This only comes after we become born again and trust him as Savior. For when we do, we become indwelt by the Holy Spirit of God, which can calm us and cause rejoicing deep within. This is especially true when we are talking about guilt in this life over our former sins.

This is not as obvious to everyone, especially those with an antinomian view of God's law. Antinomianism is a view that sees God's law as unnecessary for the Christian life. The antinomian takes the gospel's promises to the extreme and is so focused on grace that they neglect the necessity of obedience in sanctification. An antinomian would see a Christian as forgiven and who can do what he wants simply because of God's grace. It is a view that neglects repentance and the standards of holiness that come from the Scriptures. This view comes from an aversion to legalism. Legalism is the view that obedience to the law is everything, including salvation. So, the antinomian neglects the law while the legalist worships the law. Both views are extremes and unhealthy for genuine spiritual growth.

Without a proper perspective on the law, we cannot know how to live or what God requires of us as his people. The law is necessary because, as Paul says, it's our schoolmaster who points us to Christ (see Galatians 3:24-26) and shows us our need for salvation. However, the law of God also serves similarly as a speed limit sign, showing us the guidelines for what God expects of us. Without the law, we don't know what sin is nor do we know our need to be saved as sinners. Also, without God's law as Christians, we wouldn't know what we ought to do to please God and live the life that God expects of his children who are becoming like him. For you see, the law of God reflects God's character and nature. It is his holy revealed will that tells us all about him.

However, the law by itself is dangerous. If we only had the law that told us that we needed to be saved, we would be condemned and hopeless, for we would know that we were sinners but wouldn't have a way of escape. If we only had the law as a speed limit sign, then we'd question the necessity of why it's there in the first place. This is why we need more than the law. Yes, we need the law, but we must also have the gospel. As Martin Luther once said, "The law gives the diagnosis, but the gospel gives the cure."[47] Or, in the context of what we are discussing in this book, it is the law of God that tells us that we must weep for our sins, but the gospel tells us that we can weep no more. Some preach a message of "weep no more" to people who don't understand they must first weep, repent, and turn to Christ. How cruel is it to only give half the answer to the dying soul? The opposite is true; some preach only a message of "weep some more" without the gospel or hope. That is no gospel at all.

As we saw in our last chapter, weeping, which leads to a brokenness over sin, is tears that we pray will never dry up. We always want to be sensitive to sin and confess our sins and repent to God. However, for those who have repented and have been made right with God, we must now be assured of God's mercy, grace, love, and forgiveness. All who read this book, including the one who wrote it, have sinned against God. We have all failed God and have a laundry list of sins and skeletons in our closet. However, for those of

---

[47] *https://ca.thegospelcoalition.org/columns/detrinitate/martin-luther-getting-the-law-and-gospel-right/*

us who are in Christ, we must not drown in our repenting tears. God has not called you to waste your years with regret but to worship him with gratitude for his grace. So, the weeping that leads to our humility must also lead to our treasuring the gospel. Yes, there is gospel hope for weepers who are broken for their sin and who turn to Christ for forgiveness.

Again, we turn to the promise that God gave Judah during their exile. Judah had sinned until God destroyed the nation with Babylon. They then lived as captives of Babylon for 70 years before some returned to the land to rebuild the temple and the city walls. God sent them away weeping, but God encouraged them that their weeping would not be forever. Jeremiah writes, *"With weeping they shall come, and with pleas for mercy I will lead them back, I will make them walk by brooks of water, in a straight path in which they shall not stumble, for I am a father to Israel, and Ephraim is my firstborn." (Jeremiah 31:9)* He also says, *"In those days and in that time, declares the Lord, the people of Israel and the people of Judah shall come together, weeping as they come, and they shall seek the Lord their God." (Jeremiah 50:4)*

God's promises did come true, and the people returned to the land with great repentance and weeping. In the book of Ezra, we see the temple beginning to be rebuilt. The temple was the place where the glory of the Lord rested and lived among his people. It was where sacrifices for sins were made to the Lord by the priests. However, no sacrifices could no longer be made there since Nebuchadnezzar had destroyed the temple. This was the judgment of God since Judah had allowed foreign idols and great sin even into the temple. God had abandoned that place for the glory of his name and sent swift judgment to the nation. However, they were now back, and the temple was being rebuilt. What a sight that must have been to behold.

This is the way that Ezra describes it, *"And all the people shouted with a great shout when they praised the LORD because the foundation of the house of the LORD was laid. But many of the priests and Levites and heads of fathers' houses, old men who had seen the first house, wept with a loud voice when they saw the foundation of this house being laid, though many shouted aloud for joy so that the people could not distinguish the sound of the joyful shout from the sound of the people's weeping, for the people shouted with a great shout, and the sound was heard far away."* (Ezra 3:11–13)

As they laid the temple's foundation, they wept bitterly over the sins that had made its destruction necessary. However, did they stay in their sorrow? No, for it soon turned to praise and worship as they reminded themselves of God's faithful covenant love. When they saw the foundation laid, the old men who had seen the original building wept for joy. The weeping was so loud that it could be heard from far away! The theme of weeping and hope continues as we turn to the end of Ezra. Ezra learns that the people had sinned again by intermarrying the people of the land. God had forbidden this in his law (Deuteronomy 7:3-4; Ezra 9:1-2). As a result, Ezra called for a national assembly to confess and repent of their sins. In Ezra 10, we read, *"While Ezra prayed and made confession, weeping and casting himself down before the house of God, a very great assembly of men, women, and children, gathered to him out of Israel, for the people wept bitterly. And Shecaniah, the son of Jehiel, of the sons of Elam, addressed Ezra: "We have broken faith with our God and have married foreign women from the peoples of the land, but even now there is hope for Israel in spite of this." (Ezra 10:1-2)* Shecaniah knew that although they had sinned, and their sin had led to weeping, there was still hope for them despite their great sin. The same is true for us, brothers and sisters.

This message of hope is also found in the New Testament as well. James encourages his readers, *"Draw near to God, and he will draw near to you. Cleanse your hands, you sinners, and purify your hearts, you double-minded. Be wretched and mourn and weep. Let your laughter be turned to mourning and your joy to gloom." (James 4:8-9)* Ah yes, you who beat yourselves up always for your sins from previous years, may you weep for your sin, but then may your weeping lead to joy. But why can we do this? Why can we rejoice after the law has beat us up? It's because the gospel brings healing. It's because the love of God far surpasses our most significant failures and weaknesses. As the great Puritan pastor Richard Sibbes once wrote, "There is more mercy in Christ than sin in us."[48]

We can weep no more because our understanding of the law has condemned us as sinners, but the gospel of Jesus Christ has declared us righteous by faith. This is why Paul writes, *"Wretched man that I am! Who will deliver me from this body of death? Thanks be to God through Jesus Christ our Lord! So then, I myself serve the law of God with my mind, but with my flesh I serve the law of sin. There is therefore now no condemnation for those who are in Christ Jesus." (Romans 7:24-8:1)* Paul begins with his wretchedness but ends with his standing in Christ. Therefore, we can weep no more!

This truth is beautifully seen in the parable of the prodigal son in Luke 15. This is a beautiful story of repentance and restoration. Jesus told the parable of two sons, one of whom asked for his inheritance early. He wanted to leave home and forsake his father but wasn't afraid to take his father's money. When he left the house, he lived in great sin and lived recklessly. He wasted his entire inheritance in just a short time and

---

[48] *Sibbes, Richard The Bruised Reed and Smoking Flax. Reprint; Banner of Truth, 1998., pg 13*

was soon destitute. He was so desperate that, at one point, he was willing to eat what pigs ate. Remember that Jesus is telling this story to Jews who have been commanded that pigs are unclean. This would've been an abomination and of great disgust to a Jew. At this point, the young man realizes what a fool he has been leaving home and squandering his inheritance. This leads to his confession and repentance. He said, "*I will arise and go to my father, and I will say to him, "Father, I have sinned against heaven and before you. I am no longer worthy to be called your son. Treat me as one of your hired servants."* While on his way home, his father sees him coming and is filled with joy at his return. The father ran and embraced his son before the son could even say anything. How does the father respond? Does he say, "I told you so!" No, he says, *"bring quickly the best robe, and put it on him, and put a ring on his hand, and shoes on his feet. And bring the fattened calf and kill it, and let us eat and celebrate. For this my son was dead, and is alive again; he was lost, and is found.' And they began to celebrate."* (Luke 15:22–24)

What we struggle with often, when we can't stop weeping over our former sins, is what I have referred to in my life as gospel amnesia. This happens when we forget the assurance that the gospel has given to us in Christ. The assurance of our salvation is one of the most precious gifts that we can possess. Our assurance that we are forgiven in Christ alone is a hope that can help us endure all sorts of struggles and guilt that may come our way. As a pastor, I have often counseled people who had lost their assurance because they could no longer see the Savior because of deep guilt. When we lose our assurance, guilt for former sins becomes an unsurmountable hill to climb. How do we lose such assurance? I believe this happens when we become complacent about reminding ourselves of the gospel. We become afflicted with gospel amnesia.

A wonderful illustration of this is found in the *Pilgrim's Progress*. On his journey, Christian stops for a rest in the "Pleasant Arbor." This was only meant to be a momentary rest, but Christian became complacent and fell asleep. While he was asleep, his roll, which symbolized his assurance, fell off him and rolled away unnoticed. When Christian awoke, he continued his journey only to realize soon afterward that he was without his roll. How did he respond to losing his roll (assurance?) "Then was Christian in great distress and knew not what to do; for he wanted that which used to relieve him, and that which should have been his pass into the Celestial City. Here, therefore, he began to be much perplexed, and knew not what to do."[49] How true this has been in my life, and I'm sure in yours as well. Complacency to confess sin, be in the Word, be

---

[49] *Bunyan, John, Pilgrim's Progress, Moody Bible Institute (Chicago, Il) 2007 edition, pg 59*

with my church family, etc., often leads to feelings of guilt and apathy, just as Christian lost his "roll" during his sleep, we do in ours as well. So, what do you do when you lose something? Well, of course, you try to find it! However, that search for that assurance is often met with weeping and sorrow as was Christian's search for his "roll."

"But all the way he went back, who can sufficiently set forth the sorrow of Christian's heart? Sometimes he sighed, sometimes he wept, and oftentimes he chided himself for being so foolish to fall asleep in that place, which was erected only for a little refreshment from his weariness. Thus, therefore, he went back, carefully looking on this side and on that, all the way as he went, if, happily, he might find his roll that had been his comfort so many times in his journey. He went thus till he came again within sight of the arbor where he sat and slept; but that sight renewed his sorrow the more, by bringing again, even afresh, his evil of sleeping unto his mind."[50] Once gospel amnesia sets in, which causes us to lose our assurance, we will greatly sorrow and weep and be laden with even more guilt than we had before. The closer Christian got to the arbor, where he lost his roll, the guiltier he became.

---

[50] *Bunyan, John, Pilgrim's Progress, Moody Bible Institute (Chicago, Il) 2007 edition, pg 60*

Did Christian find his roll? Yes, he did, and he found it by "providence." He returned to where he had lost it and put it back into his bosom. "For this roll was the assurance of his life, and acceptance at the desired haven. Therefore, he laid it up in his bosom, gave thanks to God for directing his eyes to the place where it lay, and with joy and tears betook himself again to his journey."[51] To regain that assurance we had lost we must return to the place in which we lost it. We need to confess whatever sin it was that caused us to lose it in the first place and weep over it. It is there that by God's providence, he can direct our hearts to the place where our assurance is found, in Christ alone. Then, once we cast our eyes on Christ, we can continue in our journey with joy and not sorrow.

We often lose our assurance and live with guilt when we consider the gospel just to be our ticket to heaven and not our identity. The gospel is not just something we have received; it is where we stand before God now. The way to stop weeping for our former sins is to stop living with a "ticket" mentality. We have not just been given a ticket into a celestial city but a brand-new form of identification. A ticket is a one-time thing needed to gain access to an event. We have not been invited to an event but to eternal life.

---

[51] *Bunyan, John, Pilgrim's Progress, Moody Bible Institute (Chicago, Il) 2007 edition, pg 60*

When we do this, we miss out on the joy the gospel gives us now! Gospel amnesia is forgetting our identity in Christ and dwelling on the "old" us. We forget that the freedom, hope, rest, acceptance, and love that the Gospel gives us each day is ours to behold now. Yes, we can weep no more because of the hope of the gospel of Christ. He has forgiven us who have trusted in him for salvation. He no longer holds our sins against us. The weeping that led to much sorrow must now lead to celebration, for we are likened to the son who was dead but is now found. If the Father is celebrating, shouldn't we celebrate with him?

I love the last verse of the song, *In Christ Alone*.

"No guilt in life, no fear in death,
This is the power of Christ in me;
From life's first cry to final breath,
Jesus commands my destiny.
No power of hell, no scheme of man,
Can ever pluck me from His hand:
Till He returns or calls me home,
Here in the power of Christ I'll stand."[52]

---

[52] *gettymusic.com*

May this be our banner as we realize the hope of the gospel. We can weep no more for former sins because we are in Jesus Christ!

> Although you feel as if your pain will never end,
> Let me give you some assurance, my friend,
> The Lion of the Tribe of Judah has won the war,
> And for this reason, you will one day weep no more.

DISCUSSION QUESTIONS

1. In what ways can we avoid "gospel amnesia" and continually embrace our identity in Christ?

2. How can we encourage one another to move from a place of weeping and sorrow over sin to a place of celebration and joy in Christ?

3. What practical steps can we take to keep the gospel central in our lives and avoid falling into the extremes of legalism or antinomianism?

4. How does the promise of no condemnation in Christ (Romans 8:1) impact your daily life and interactions with others?

5. How does the example of Judah's exile and return, as described in the book of Jeremiah and Ezra, illustrate the relationship between weeping over sin and experiencing God's restoration and mercy?

6. Can you relate to Christian in *The Pilgrim's Progress?* Have you ever lost your assurance of salvation after a time of spiritual complacency?

CHAPTER 14:
THE END OF WEEPING?

I love to watch a good movie. When I say a "good" movie, let me clarify that I love unpredictable movies. I like it when I'm surprised by the ending or an unexpected plot twist. I get so bored if I can figure out what the movie will be about before it begins. I love the feeling of being shocked by something unexpected. Perhaps this is why I love science fiction movies. I don't want to see a movie about things that happen in my ordinary life. I want to explore beyond what is possible and dream about something that, for example: "happened a long time ago in a galaxy far, far away." Those kinds of movies are the best! Have you ever been watching a movie and were just dying for it to end? Once I'm bored with a movie, I keep looking at the clock and start counting down the minutes before I can move on with the rest of my life. I am a little dramatic here, but maybe I'm not completely. The point is that you never want to end a "good" movie! You can watch it for hours and not get bored of it. As for a "bad" movie, you may want it to end as quickly as possible.

Why do I bring up my taste in movies? Well, I believe it applies to our discussion throughout this book. We have lived diffcrent lives with various amounts of weeping. Some may view their lives as a "bad" movie, which is understandable. They may look at all the tears and can't wait for the pain to end. Some may eagerly anticipate for the credits of their life to roll so they can go home. Not everyone has their sorrows resolved in this life. For many, the weeping lasts a lifetime because some wounds are too deep to recover from in our fallen condition. I understand why you await those credits to roll so you can move on. Whether or not the plot is resolved before you die, it will all be resolved. Of course, this promise only applies to believers.

The weeping will never end for those who don't believe and trust in Christ alone. There is no such thing as R.I.P. "resting in peace" for those who die in their sins. Jesus told a parable to describe the separation of the righteous from the wicked on judgment day. Jesus says, *"Again, the kingdom of heaven is like a net that was thrown into the sea and gathered fish of every kind. When it was full, men drew it ashore and sat down and sorted the good into containers but threw away the bad. So it will be at the end of the age. The angels will come out and separate the evil from the righteous and throw them into the fiery furnace. In that place there will be weeping and gnashing of teeth." (Matthew 13:47-50)* Jesus refers to hell as a place where there is *"weeping and gnashing of teeth"* in several locations (Matthew 8:12, 22:13, 24:51, 25:30, Luke 13:28).

Jesus also told a parable about a rich man and a man named Lazarus. Both these men died but went to different places. Lazarus died and went to "Abraham's side," also known as paradise. The rich man died but went to "Hades." Hades signified the unrighteous compartment of the grave, or, as we call it, hell. Jesus said that when this man died, he was in *"torment."* He is pleading for mercy and begging Lazarus to give him some relief. He says, *"Abraham, have mercy on me, and send Lazarus to dip the end of his finger in water and cool my tongue, for I am in anguish in this flame."* (Luke 16:24) Both men experienced two different realities after their death. One of these realities was "comfort," and the other was "anguish" (See Luke 16:25). Lazarus was in a place where all his pain, discomforts, and sorrows were erased. The rich man, however, only had the sorrows of his life amplified to infinite levels. Hell is a sobering reality to consider as sinners face the wrath of God if they die in their sins.

When unbelievers die now, they instantly go to hell and receive everlasting judgment for their sins. However, hell is not the final resting place for those who die without Jesus. In Revelation 20, John saw a vision of the great white throne judgment. *"Then I saw a great white throne and him who was seated on it. From his presence earth and sky fled away, and no place was found for them. And I saw the dead, great and small, standing before the throne, and books were opened. Then another book was opened, which is the book of life. And the dead were judged by what was written in the books, according to what they had done. And the sea gave up the dead who were in it, Death and Hades gave up the dead who were in them, and they were judged, each one of them, according to what they had done. Then Death and Hades were thrown into the lake of fire. This is the second death, the lake of fire. And if anyone's name was not found written in the book of life, he was thrown into the lake of fire." (Revelation 20:11–15)* Hell will deliver all those who died to stand before God, and they will all be thrown into the Lake of Fire. In the Lake of Fire, sinners spend an eternity facing the wrath of sinning against an infinitely Holy God.

The Lake of Fire will be filled with weepers who find no rest and are tormented forever. They will face an infinite amount of crying, mourning, pain, and death. Yes, this is the opposite of those redeemed by the Lamb, for those in the Lake of Fire experience eternal death. Hell is more than just a curse word that we utter flippantly in this life. It will be a place where the justice of God is honored and upheld for all those who rejected to be saved by grace. This should make us weep in this life, friends. This should encourage our evangelism! This should make us want to support more missionaries! For Jesus is worthy of receiving worship by every human being on earth. None of the things I have written in this book about the promises of God apply to those who reject Christ. This will be far worse than watching a bad movie that seemingly never ends. They will want it to end, but it won't. Jesus describes it as being *"eternal punishment" (Matthew 25:46)*. It is a place where the *"worm does not die and the fire is not quenched." (Mark 9:48)* It will be a place with *"no rest"* (Revelation 14:11). Those who die rejecting Christ will never know what it means to "weep no more." They will weep forevermore!

R.C. Sproul wrote, "Perhaps the most frightening aspect of hell is its eternality. People can endure the greatest agony if they know it will ultimately stop. In hell there is no such hope. The Bible clearly teaches that the punishment is eternal. The same word is used for both eternal life and eternal death. Punishment implies pain. Mere annihilation, which some have lobbied for, involves no pain."[53] Also Jonathan Edwards once preached that "Wicked men will hereafter earnestly wish to be turned to nothing and forever cease to be that they may escape the wrath of God."[54]

Friends, why do you delay your repentance? Why do you play games with God? Repent and trust in

---

[53] *https://www.bible-researcher.com/hell6.html*

[54] *Gerstner, John Jonathan Edwards on Heaven and Hell, Orlando: Ligonier Ministries, 1991, 75*

Christ to save you now! He died in your place, was buried, and rose again from the dead. Confess your sins to God and trust Jesus as the only one worthy to die for your sins. You can't do anything to save yourself. Your good works and money are worthless before a Holy God. You owe God a debt you can never pay back. Humble yourself and acknowledge that Jesus is the only way you can escape God's wrath and your eternal weeping. Believe in what he has done for you is all you need, and you will be saved. If you reject the truth of the gospel and don't want Christ to save you, then you will keep on weeping, and it will never end. Believe that Jesus died on the cross for your sins, was buried, and rose again. If you die as an unbeliever, there is no hope in the grave for you. There is no salvation after death. The Word of God says so, *"And just as it is appointed for man to die once, and after that comes judgment." (Hebrews 9:27)* Or as Puritan pastor George Swinnock wrote about the death of unbelievers, "Against this arrest there is no bail."[55]

However, if you trust this Christ and believe in him, then all the promises of this book will come to fruition. You will not be cast into hell but will reign with Christ in a new heaven and a new earth. It is a world you have longed for through every tear your eyes

---

[55] *Smith, Dale W, Ore from the Puritans' Mine, Reformation Heritage Books, Grand Rapids, MI) 2020, pg. 118*

have shed. In this place, your weeping will forever end. John writes, *"He will wipe away every tear from their eyes, and death shall be no more, neither shall there be mourning, nor crying, nor pain anymore, for the former things have passed away." (Revelation 21:4)* What is this new world? The Bible describes it as a new heaven and a new earth. *"Then I saw a new heaven and a new earth, for the first heaven and the first earth had passed away, and the sea was no more." (Revelation 21:1)* In this new world, it will be as if you're watching a movie that you never want to end. The good news is that it's far better than any movie could ever be. It is real and will never end. This new world will be where you can't hurt or be hurt again, where sorrow and sadness do not exist. We currently live in a world where sin dwells and is ubiquitous. However, it won't always be like that, for God has promised that new days are coming. Peter writes, *"But according to his promise we are waiting for new heavens and a new earth in which righteousness dwells." (2 Peter 3:13)*

    Christian encounters this reality as he concludes his journey in the *Pilgrim's Progress*. As he reaches the gates of the Celestial City, he inquires what there is to do there. He is told that he will "there receive the comfort of all your toil and have joy for all your sorrow; you must reap what you have sown, even the fruit of all your prayers, and tears, and sufferings for the King by the way."[56] Oh yes, doesn't that sound heavenly, dear friends? Yes, there will be comfort for all our toil. There will be joy for all our sorrows. We will also reap all the fruit that our tears had been producing all the days of our pain and sorrow. It is when we reach this place that we will realize that there were no wasted tears. It is here that we will understand that all of suffering and sorrows were not for nothing and were used by King Jesus for our good. I can't wait for this day to come. How about you?

How does this happen? How does this world go from one full of tears to one where all tears will be gone? The answer is in Peter's description: "righteousness" dwells in this world. As previously mentioned, there is evil all around us in our present world. However, no evil, darkness, or even one impure motive will exist in this new world, meaning there is no sin. Where there is no sin, there are no sinners to sin. This is how John describes this new heaven and new earth. *"But nothing unclean will ever enter it, nor anyone who does what is detestable or false, but only those who are found written in the Lamb's book of life." (Revelation 21:27)*

Since sin is eliminated from this new world, it only makes sense that the wages of sin must also cease to exist. The wages of sin, according to the Apostle

---

[56] *Bunyan, John, Pilgrim's Progress, Moody Bible Institute (Chicago, Il) 2007 edition, pg*

Paul, is death (See Romans 3:23). Death will be no more! So, then we must ask the question: when does death die? When will this new world be here? When death dies, it will end all weeping and crying for those redeemed by the Lamb of God. According to Scripture, death will die at the Second Coming of the Lord Jesus when he delivers the Kingdom to God the Father. Paul wrote to the Corinthians, *"Then comes the end, when he delivers the kingdom of God the Father after destroying every rule and every authority and power. For he must reign until he has put all his enemies under his feet. The last enemy to be destroyed is death." (1 Corinthians 15:24-26)*

Without sin in this new world, there are no wages to pay. Therefore, death goes bankrupt, is out of business, and will never be seen again. Death was born when Adam sinned against God, and it will die when the second Adam (Jesus) returns in glory (see 1 Corinthians 15:45-49). The resurrection of Christ is the evidence that he has truly conquered death and will one day end it. This is why John says, *"He will wipe away every tear from their eyes, and death shall be no more, neither shall there be mourning, nor crying, nor pain anymore, for the former things have passed away." (Revelation 21:4)*

Sin brings forth death. Death brings forth crying and pain. If you eliminate sin, you eliminate everything else that results from it. There is a day when God removes this curse from creation, and it will be impossible to sin. If sin can't exist in this new world, it's impossible for weeping to exist. This is the promise that God has given to those who weep. Weeping is for now, but it is not forever if you are in Jesus Christ. Your tears serve a purpose now, but one day, your tears will no longer be needed.

This is not just a new promise that God gives us at the end of the book of Revelation. The Old Testament contains similar promises. Isaiah prophesied, *"He will swallow up death forever, and the Lord God will wipe away tears from all faces, and the reproach of his people he will take away from all the earth, for the Lord has spoken."* (Isaiah 25:8) Here it is again in Isaiah's prophecy, the end of death signals the end of tears. When God destroys death, he will also take away the shame that those tears brought on his people. God also told Isaiah, *"I will rejoice in Jerusalem and be glad in my people; no more shall be heard in it the sound of weeping and the cry of distress."* (Isaiah 65:19) Of course, this was coming at a time when there was so much sin and sorrow in the land. Judah had been disobedient to God and was facing judgment. King Nebuchadnezzar of Babylon was coming to kill many, and the rest who survived would soon be enslaved. However, God did not send them to Babylon without promises. Isaiah wrote to them, considering the coming judgment, *"For a people shall dwell in Zion, in Jerusalem; you shall weep no more. He will surely be gracious to you at the sound of your cry. As soon as he hears it, he answers you." (Isaiah 30:19)* Yes, weep no more was also an Old Testament promise that finds its fulfillment in Christ alone.

Jesus also gave this hope to his followers and the crowds during his earthly ministry. In the sermon on the mount, Jesus preached, *"Blessed are you who are hungry now, for you shall be satisfied. Blessed are you who weep now, for you shall laugh." (Luke 6:21)* Jesus also told his disciples, *"Truly, truly, I say to you, you will weep and lament, but the world will rejoice. You will be sorrowful, but your sorrow will turn into joy." (John 16:20)* God's promises to his people have always included a promise for the end of weeping.

Therefore, even though crying is therapeutic and helpful for now, there will be a day when it will no longer be needed to calm our hearts or to express the pain that resides within. I don't know about you, but I long for that day. I long for the day in which all this wickedness, pain, evil, sorrow, and grief will end as the wages of sin breathe their last. I'm longing for the day that my sin can no longer be found as something done by me in the present. Right now, I stand with a verdict of *"no condemnation"* (Romans 8:1), but my sin still brings me sorrow for myself and sorrow for others. Although I stand righteous in Jesus Christ, I still partake in the evil of this world as I battle my sinful nature. I am confident that my many sorrows will soon be defeated. My sanctification is in progress, which makes my need for repentance perpetual, and as God grows me in holiness, I should sin less and less, but I still sin, nonetheless. My sin will lead to my death as it is the just wages that I have earned for myself in this life, but I will be raised in Him never to sin or die again. This is why, in our weeping, our victory rests in the Lamb of God. Our weeping will soon be conquered by the Lamb, who was worthy to open the seals to signal the end of John's suffering and ours. Take courage, my friend, for you will one day, weep no more!

> Although you feel as if your pain will never end,
> Let me give you some assurance, my friend,
> The Lion of the Tribe of Judah has won the war,
> And for this reason, you will one day weep no more.

DISCUSSION QUESTIONS

1. Reflecting on the description of hell as a place of eternal weeping and gnashing of teeth, how does this imagery impact your understanding of the consequences of rejecting God's grace? How does it challenge you to share your faith with those who don't know?

2. Reflect on the idea that death will be no more in the new heavens and new earth. How does this promise impact your understanding of life's ultimate purpose and meaning?

3. How does the promise of an end to weeping in the new creation offer hope and assurance to those who are currently experiencing sorrow and pain? How can this promise bring comfort in times of grief?

4. How can we live considering the hope of heaven, embracing life's uncertainties and challenges with faith and trust in God's promises?

5. Are you a Christian? Do the promises of this book apply to you? Will your weeping end? Or will it last forevermore? How do you know?

Made in the USA
Columbia, SC
01 July 2024